# 40 Hill, Glen & Coastal Walks

The author and publisher have made every effort to ensure that the information in this publication is accurate, and accept no responsibility whatsoever for any loss, injury or inconvenience experienced by any person or persons whilst using this book.

*For Andy Godfrey and Giulia Hetherington, island-going comrades par excellence!*

published by
**pocket mountains ltd**
The Old Church, Annanside, Moffat,
Dumfries and Galloway DG10 9HB
www.pocketmountains.com

ISBN: 978-1-916739-19-2



A catalogue record for this book is available from the British Library



Printed by J Thomson Colour Printers, Glasgow

# Introduction

Lying between the Ayrshire coast and the Kintyre Peninsula, the Isle of Arran (Scottish Gaelic: *Eilean Arainn*) is the largest island in the Firth of Clyde at 432 sq km with a population of around 4600. Often referred to as 'Scotland in miniature', Arran is divided geographically and geologically into highland and lowland areas by the Highland Boundary Fault; the mountainous north of the island contains ridges that rival anything in the Highlands, while rolling moorland, forestry and farmland predominate in the south.

This guidebook brings together 40 of the island's best walking routes, from strolls along Arran's southern shores and visits to waterfalls, lochs and ancient monuments to day-long mountain ridge traverses and rugged coastal walks.

Arran is relatively compact with good public transport, making the island easy to explore. The routes in this book are divided into five sections, each of which is introduced by a summary overview of the area and a map showing their locations.

### History

Arran's landscape is littered with historical remains, both ancient and more recent. Neolithic hunters and farmers left few traces of their settlements except a number of immense chambered burial mounds known as Clyde cairns, particularly in the south of the island. Examples include the Giants' Graves overlooking Whiting Bay and Torrylin Cairn at Kilmory.

Traces of Bronze Age culture include hut circles, stone circles and smaller burial cairns, with the best examples found around Machrie Moor and Blackwaterfoot. These traces and monuments bear the hallmark of settled well-organised communities. Many Iron Age hillforts – or duns – are also found, predominantly in the south of the island, their presence suggesting some degree of insecurity or conflict during this era.

During the 6th century, Gaelic-speakers from Ireland, including early Celtic Christian missionaries, arrived on Arran as they colonised Argyll and the islands of the western seaboard. The scattered kingdom, known as Dalriada, became a stronghold of the Gaelic language and the culture of the Gaels.

Arran came under Norse control in 1098 which lasted until 1156 when Somerled, the Norse-Gael warlord, led a force against the Norsemen and became ruler of old Dalriada. The Norse territories were ceded to the Kingdom of Scotland at the Treaty of Perth in 1266. Somerled's descendants, Clan Donald – known as the Lords of the Isles – emerged as the dominant power, ruling the isles until 1493.

Following a tumultuous period during the Scottish Wars of Independence, Brodick Castle was granted to James Hamilton by James III at the end of the 15th century. The Hamilton family resided on Arran for several centuries, overseeing the gradual population growth before the

10th Duke of Hamilton instigated a devastating programme of Clearances in the early 19th century. In scenes repeated throughout the Highlands and Islands, whole villages were displaced in favour of sheep and the Gaelic culture of the island was devastated. The population was either resettled in purpose-built cottages or forced to emigrate to Canada and other parts of the New World.

**Natural history**

Arran has a great range of wildlife to see. Otters have territories around the coastline and may be spotted hunting in the shallows. Common seals can be seen basking on rocky and bouldery parts of the shore. Herds of red deer roam the hills and glens in the island's north and are subject to culling to control numbers – be aware that stag stalking takes place between mid-August and mid-October. Red squirrels can be spotted on woodland walks around Arran and brown hares can be seen in the south of the island.

The island is home to various reptiles, including adders, common lizards and slow worms. Salmon, trout and even carp are among the species present in Arran's rivers and freshwater lochs.

Dragonflies, damselflies, butterflies and moths are plentiful in the summer, but the milder weather can also bring swarms of midges – strong sunshine, a stiff breeze and plenty of repellent are the antidotes. Clegs – a small aggressive horsefly – and deer ticks add to the list of hugely annoying small biting beasties.

Golden eagles, hawks and ravens haunt the mountains and uplands. Red grouse are populous in the southern moorlands while black grouse are an introduced species. Barn owls, long- and short-eared owls and tawny owls are all present. Varied coastal habitats support a plethora of ducks, waders and divers, as well as many types of gull. Ailsa Craig is home to a huge gannet colony and they can be seen diving spectacularly for fish all around Arran. Herons are found along riverbanks and the seashore, especially in wooded areas.

**Weather**

The weather on the west coast of Scotland is famously changeable, so it's best to prepare for all eventualities; pack warm layers and waterproofs year round, as well as sun block and a sun hat in summer.

The mild oceanic climate of the west coast keeps temperatures generally cool. The summer months are relatively mild and windy; the winters are cold, wet and very windy. May and June are typically the island's sunniest months, though July and August are the warmest. December through February are the coldest months.

In common with other islands of Scotland's western seaboard, annual rainfall is high and this is particularly the case in the mountainous north. The east coast is more sheltered from prevailing winds than the island's south and west.

Snow seldom lies at sea level and frosts are less frequent than on the mainland; however, snow and ice are a possibility in Arran's mountains between September and April – so it is important to be properly equipped when heading into the hills.

Check weather forecasts before setting out on walks, but be aware that the actual weather doesn't always correspond and prepare accordingly.

**Access and safety**

Public access to the countryside is a statutory right in Scotland. The Scottish Outdoor Access Code gives guidance for those exercising their right to roam and land managers (outdooraccess-scotland.scot). Walkers have the right to roam over all open land contingent on treating the environment and wildlife with care, respecting the needs and privacy of those living and working in the countryside and avoiding obstructing activities such as farming, crofting and deer stalking. Dogs must be kept under close control around livestock or ground-nesting birds.

Allow plenty of time to complete walks, and always let someone know your intended route and estimated time of completion. While some of the routes featured here follow clear paths and tracks, others follow vague and intermittent paths at best, requiring a degree of navigational competence. Many of the walks in this guidebook are suitable for all ages and abilities, but there are also a number of hillwalking routes that are best suited to fit, experienced walkers. Arran's northern hills make for some fantastic walking with tremendous views, but can be very exposed and difficult to navigate in inclement weather.

**Getting there and getting around**

Arran is close to the busy transport hub of Glasgow with good onward road and rail links to Ardrossan Harbour for the ferry service to Brodick. A ferry also runs to Lochranza from Claonaig on the Kintyre peninsula in summer and Tarbert (Loch Fyne) in winter. Sailings are frequent in summer with a reduced service in winter. Both ferries carry vehicles.

There is an extensive bus service on Arran, departing from Brodick ferry terminal and running around the island all day, although the Sunday service is much reduced. All of the walks here can be accessed by bus with at most a short walk to the start. Drivers should be aware that roads are often narrow and winding with few passing places. Plenty of walkers and cyclists are also encountered on the roads – as are sheep and deer on occasion.

Arran is circumnavigated by a 90km-long mostly coastal road, with minor roads along the western side, linking most of the island's settlements. Arran's other two roads run across the island from east to west – The String from Brodick to Blackwaterfoot and The Ross from Lamlash to Lagg.

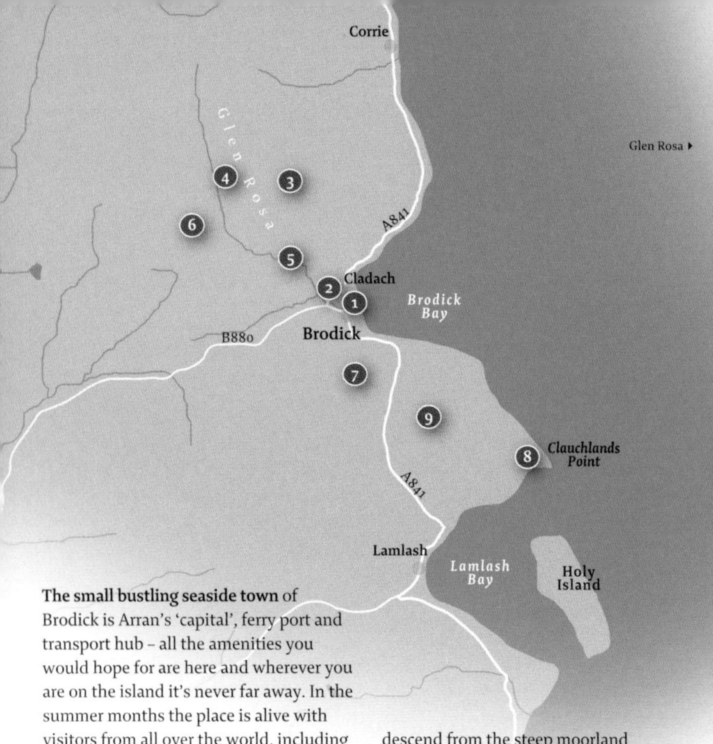


**The small bustling seaside town** of Brodick is Arran's 'capital', ferry port and transport hub – all the amenities you would hope for are here and wherever you are on the island it's never far away. In the summer months the place is alive with visitors from all over the world, including many cheery daytrippers from Glasgow.

Unsurprisingly, Brodick makes a well-connected starting point for most of the walks in this area of the island. Straight from the ferry there are coastal walks, woodland walks and numerous sites of historical interest that can be visited on foot, including Brodick Castle with its fine formal gardens on the wooded slopes of Goatfell – Arran's highest peak, which rises imperiously to the north of Brodick Bay.

Wooded glens and tumbling burns descend from the steep moorland escarpment to the west of the town while to the south Brodick is bordered by forested hillsides and the heathery Clauchland Hills. Hill walks in this area include the ever-popular route from Cladach to the summit of Goatfell and the horseshoe ridge walk encompassing the Three Beinns – Beinn Nuis, Beinn Tarsuinn and Beinn a' Chliabhain. There are also low-level walks along Brodick Bay, through beautiful Glen Rosa and around Clauchlands Point to name a few.

# Brodick and Glen Rosa

# The Fisherman's Walk

**Distance 5.5km Time 2 hours**
**Terrain gravel and grassy tracks, sandy shore, woodland paths and minor roads**
**Map OS Explorer 361 Access Brodick is the island's bus terminus**

**Head north from Brodick around the bay with its fine sandy beach to reach the grounds of Brodick Castle and Country Park. The return follows paths and minor roads inland, passing a variety of island enterprises and the Arran Heritage Museum. The outward leg of this walk is often used as the approach to the most popular route up Goatfell.**

Start from the shoreside Invercloy car park. From the ferry terminal, this is off the A841 northbound; a blue sign indicates the Fisherman's Walk. From the car park, take the path between the shore and a play park. There are fine views across Brodick Bay towards the castle in its woodland setting, with Goatfell towering above.

Cross the footbridge over the Glencloy Water and follow the boardwalk skirting between saltmarsh and shore, crossing another footbridge. Go through a gate and follow the path crossing a corner of the golf course – give way to golfers. At a path junction, bear right to cross the golf club footbridge across Glenrosa Water, then turn sharply right as advised by a warning sign and follow the riverbank downstream. The path leads through aromatic gorse alongside the golf course for a short distance, before emerging on the sandy shoreline of Brodick's northern beach where you continue until a short

boardwalk on the left takes you to a footbridge across the Cnocan Burn.

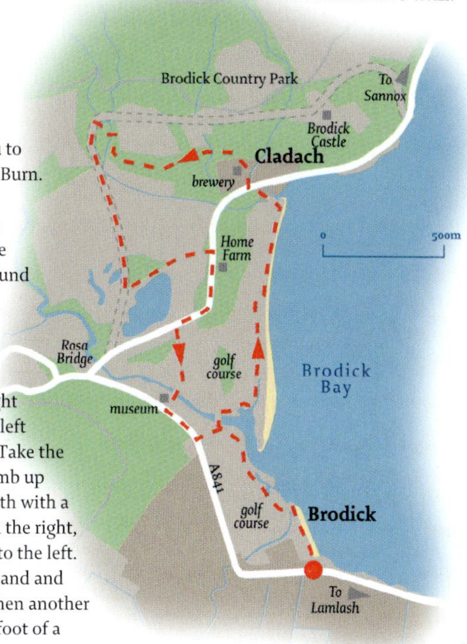

Cross this into an area of woodland to reach the car park beside the A841. This is also the start point for walks in and around Glen Rosa, the most popular route up Goatfell and the Brodick Castle forest trails.

Cross the road with care and take the track leading to the right of the restaurant, then bearing left past the Isle of Arran Brewery. Take the signposted Goatfell Path to climb up through woodland. Ignore a path with a purple waymarker joining from the right, then take a path branching off to the left. The path winds through woodland and crosses a wooden footbridge, then another more substantial bridge at the foot of a gorge. Turn right and then bear left, climbing up to meet a minor road with a stone-built bridge to the right. Turn left along the castle access road. Look out for gaps in a hedgerow through which can be seen several small standing stones, one in the field to the left of the road and two to the right, framed against the impressive backdrop of Glen Rosa and its surrounding rocky ridges.

Shortly after, take the track on the left, which soon leads past a picturesque pond. Keep right at a fork before emerging back on the A841 opposite Arran Aromatics and the Arran Cheese Shop. Turn right to continue along the pavement, following the main road which soon bends to the right. A short way further on, turn left to cross the road and join a cyclepath and footpath signposted for Brodick and the Heritage Museum. The path soon crosses a footbridge and rejoins the road by the Arran Heritage Museum.

Cross over to join the pavement and turn left alongside the main road, soon passing an impressive standing stone right by the roadside. By the school, turn left to cross back over the road and take a path adjacent to a parking area. The path soon rejoins the outward route at the footbridge on the golf course; turn right to continue back to Brodick.

◂ Brodick Bay

# Brodick Castle forest trails

**Distance** 3.5km **Time** 1 hour 30 **Terrain** woodland footpaths and tracks; muddy in places **Map** OS Explorer 361 **Access** bus to Cladach from Brodick

**Starting from Cladach, 1.5km north of Brodick, this undemanding short walk stitches together some of the many paths weaving around the wooded environs of Brodick Castle and Country Park. As well as the castle, there is an old burial ground and a reconstruction of a Bronze Age hut. There is an admission charge to the castle itself and its formal gardens.**

From the bus stop/car park at Cladach, follow the track north past the restaurant and the Isle of Arran Brewery. The obvious track continues uphill through woodland with signposts indicating Goatfell Path. Ignore a path to the right with a purple waymarker, then take a path forking left a short distance further on. This winds through woodland and crosses a footbridge, then a bigger bridge over the Cnocan Burn at the foot of a gorge. Turn right and then bear left, climbing up to meet a minor road with a stone-built bridge to the right. Cross straight over the road onto the path opposite.

Continue straight ahead, ignoring a path forking down to the right and keeping high above the burn flowing through a small gorge. At a fork, keep left on the higher path, then branch right (straight ahead) at the next junction where an old marker post indicates 'Goatfell

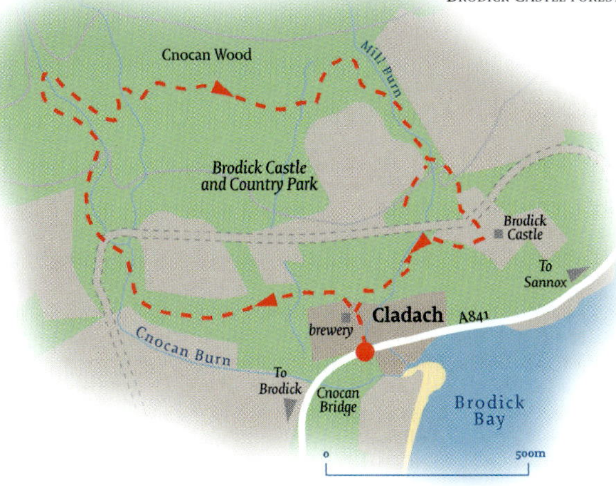


track'. Cross a substantial footbridge over the burn and at the next path junction follow the path signposted for the Goatfell track. At the junction after this, cross straight over the more prominent path, keeping ahead along a woodland path to reach a small gated cemetery. Brodick Castle is the ancient seat of the Dukes of Hamilton and this small private burial ground is the last resting place of the 11th and 12th Dukes.

The path narrows as you continue; keep right at the next junction which soon leads downhill and crosses a footbridge. The path passes close to another small gorge before crossing another footbridge. Go through an old metal gate and continue to a further footbridge; before crossing it's worth detouring along the signposted path on the right to visit the reconstruction of a Bronze Age hut. Keep left at a fork to reach the hut, which is open on certain days (there is a separate admission charge or it is also included with a castle visit ticket). Retrace your steps to cross the footbridge.

The path soon arrives at the Ranger Centre; take the path to the right, passing an adventure playground, then fork left to the rear of Brodick Castle. The castle and its formal gardens are open to the public (admission fee) and are well worth a visit. Otherwise, continue across the driveway to the near right corner of the castle, then follow a track leading down a slope to the right, which then bends to the left – a signpost indicates a detour to the Squirrel Hide here (also worth a visit as there is a good chance of seeing red squirrels). Carry on along the main path, soon passing the entrance hut with a sign indicating Exit to Cladach. Cross a bridge, fork left and take steps down to the left to return to Cladach as signposted.

◂ Brodick Castle

# Goatfell from Cladach

**Distance** 11km **Time** 4 hours
**Terrain** forest tracks, open moorland and very rough, rocky mountain terrain
**Map** OS Explorer 361 **Access** bus to Cladach from Brodick

**Arran's highest peak is so synonymous with the island itself that it would be almost rude to visit without climbing it. This route follows forest tracks before a good path leads the way across rugged open moorland onto the shoulder of Goatfell. The mountain's upper reaches are steep and bouldery, though a narrow path aids progress to the summit trig point.**

From the bus stop/car park at Cladach, take the track north past the restaurant and the Isle of Arran Brewery. The obvious track continues uphill through woodland with signposts indicating Goatfell Path. Ignore a path to the right and another to the left, cross the tarmac driveway for Brodick Castle and pass a National Trust for Scotland information panel.

Continue uphill into Forestry Commission land and keep straight ahead when the main path is intersected by waymarked trails at Cnocan. Eventually, the main path swings sharply right; leave it here to carry straight on along a rougher, narrower path, which soon leaves the woodland behind. Cross heather and

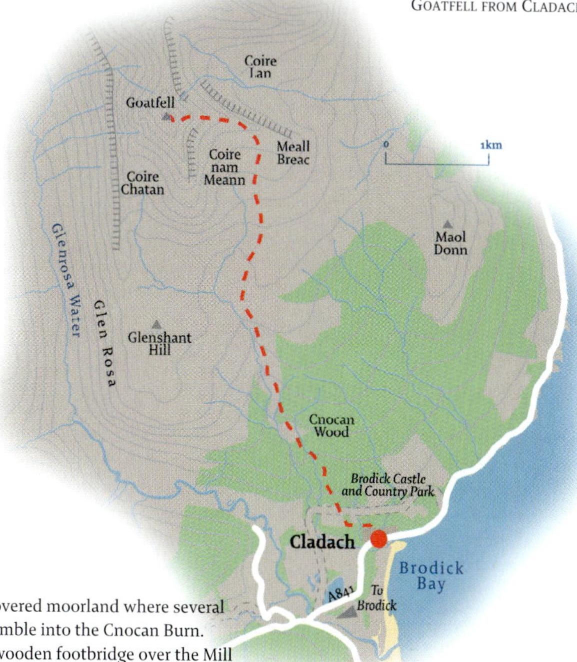


bracken-covered moorland where several streams tumble into the Cnocan Burn.

Cross a wooden footbridge over the Mill Burn, soon passing through a gate in a high deer fence. The terrain becomes more rugged, heathery and bouldery and the gradient eases for a while before rising once more to gain the shoulder on Meall Breac, where the path climbing from Corrie joins from the right. Bear left to continue steeply uphill, following the path over and between the bouldery knuckles studding the ridge. In icy conditions it is safer to traverse left of the rocky outcrop beneath the summit. Once over or around this final obstacle, the summit at 874m is gained rather suddenly.

The effort of the climb is rewarded with spectacular views, especially over the surrounding ridges and peaks to the west and north. The panorama extends eastwards across the Firth of Clyde to the Ayrshire coast with the hills of southwest Scotland beyond and as far southwest as the Antrim coast on a clear day. The summit has an OS trig point and also a view indicator. Retrace your outward route to return to Cladach, enjoying the fine views over Brodick Bay, but stay alert as it's easy to take a wrong turn in the woods.

◂ Goatfell

# Goatfell and Glen Rosa

**Distance 15.5km Time 6 hours 30 Terrain woodland and moorland paths, and rocky ridge Map OS Explorer 361 Access bus to Cladach from Brodick**

**Make a day of climbing Goatfell, continuing along the Stacach ridge to North Goatfell and returning via The Saddle and Glen Rosa for an exhilarating walk. The descent from North Goatfell involves occasional hands on and can be hazardous in icy or wet conditions.**

From the bus stop/car park at Cladach, take the track north past the restaurant and the Isle of Arran Brewery. The obvious path continues uphill through woodland with signposts indicating the Goatfell Path. Cross a tarmac driveway and carry on uphill, keeping straight ahead on the main path. Where this swings sharply right, go straight on along the rougher path to soon exit the woodland and cross heather- and bracken-covered moorland parallel to the Cnocan Burn.

After crossing a footbridge over the Mill Burn, go through a gate. The terrain becomes more rugged, then the gradient eases before rising to gain the shoulder on Meall Breac. Bear left steeply uphill, following the path over and between bouldery outcrops along the ridge. In icy conditions, it is safer to traverse left of the rocky outcrop beneath the summit. Once past this final obstacle, the 874m-high summit with its trig point and view indicator is reached suddenly, giving spectacular views over the surrounding ridges and peaks to the west and north.

Descend northwards through bouldery terrain. The path narrows as it joins the Stacach ridge linking Goatfell and North Goatfell with its series of granite tors; these can be avoided by keeping to the path beneath the outcrops on the eastern

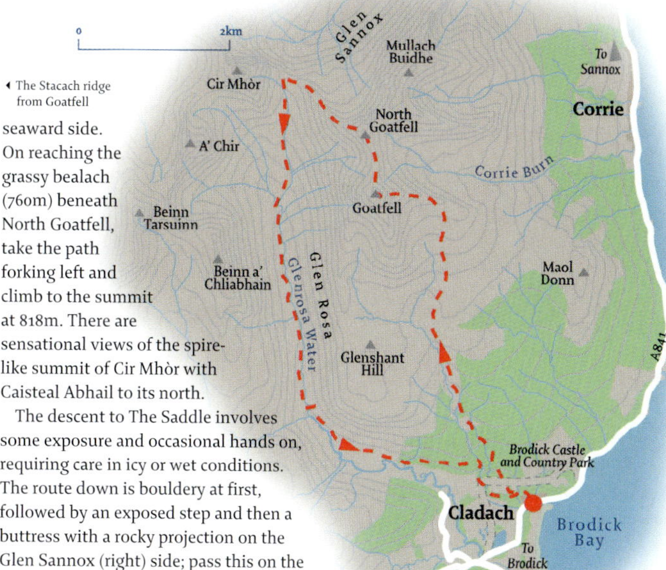


◂ The Stacach ridge from Goatfell

seaward side. On reaching the grassy bealach (760m) beneath North Goatfell, take the path forking left and climb to the summit at 818m. There are sensational views of the spire-like summit of Cir Mhòr with Caisteal Abhail to its north.

The descent to The Saddle involves some exposure and occasional hands on, requiring care in icy or wet conditions. The route down is bouldery at first, followed by an exposed step and then a buttress with a rocky projection on the Glen Sannox (right) side; pass this on the Glen Rosa side. Continue the descent on gritty slopes and a worn path along the bouldery ridge. The gradient eases before the path descends to reach the pass.

Keep on a short way beyond the lowest point of The Saddle, gaining a little height until you meet an obvious path crossing the pass. Turn left (south) and descend into Glen Rosa on a good path, following the Glenrosa Water and eventually passing through a woodland enclosure. Shortly before the confluence of the Garbh Allt and Glenrosa Water, bear left to cross a footbridge over the latter. Climb along the narrow footpath contouring along the lower slopes of Creag Rosa. Go through a gate at the edge of woodland and follow the vague path along the forest edge. Cross a gap in an old drystane dyke, turn left up a rise alongside the dyke, then right to follow the obvious grassy track as it climbs gently through the forest.

Turn right at the next path junction, descending alongside the Cnocan Burn. Continue straight over a road by a stone bridge, following the path down to a footbridge. Cross this and follow an earth track through mature woodland, going over another footbridge. At the next path junction, turn right to descend along the path and retrace your outward journey to the start.

# Glen Rosa circuit

**Distance 9.5km Time 3 hours**
**Terrain paths, gravel tracks, minor road; boggy in places Map OS Explorer 361**
**Access bus to Cladach from Brodick**

**This circular walk leads through the woodland at Cladach into beautiful Glen Rosa, cradled between rugged mountain peaks and traversed by the lovely Glenrosa Water with its waterfalls, pools and cascades.**

From the bus stop/car park at Cladach, follow the track north past the restaurant and the Isle of Arran Brewery. The obvious path continues uphill through woodland with signposts indicating the Goatfell Path. Ignore a path to the right with a purple waymarker, then take a path forking left a short way further on. Follow this earth track through mature woodland, eventually crossing a wooden footbridge, then continuing through the trees to reach a second larger footbridge. Cross over, turn right, then bear left, following the path uphill to meet a surfaced lane by a stone bridge. Cross straight over the road to continue on an obvious path which starts to climb steadily. On reaching a fork, continue uphill on the left-hand branch.

At the next path junction, turn left where a sign indicates Glen Rosa and follow the bracken-fringed path descending gradually through mixed deciduous and coniferous woodland. The path arrives at a drystane dyke on the edge of mature coniferous plantation; turn left

and follow the line of the dyke down to a path junction. Turn right through a gap in the dyke, and continue along the edge of and then through the woodland to a gate onto the open hillside.

A narrow but clear path contours along the slopes below Creag Rosa with the Glenrosa Water winding through the glen below. As the path leads further into the glen, the views become increasingly dramatic with the A' Chir ridge and Cir Mhòr dominating the head of the glen as the route turns northwards. Eventually, the path descends via some rocky steps to the Glenrosa Water where it is crossed by a footbridge. There are a number of picturesque pools and cascades along this stretch of the burn. You can carry on up Glen Rosa as far as you like, perhaps even to reach The Saddle with its views along Glens Rosa and Sannox and the mountain ridges that flank them.

The return path follows the Glenrosa Water southwards across a bridge, soon joining a more substantial track and then a surfaced road by the Glen Rosa Campsite. Follow the minor road for 1km to where it joins the B880; turn left here and continue to a junction with the A841. Turn left, cross the Rosa Bridge and follow the road for a further 1km to return to Cladach and the start of the route. There is no pavement for the first 200m, so take care on this section.

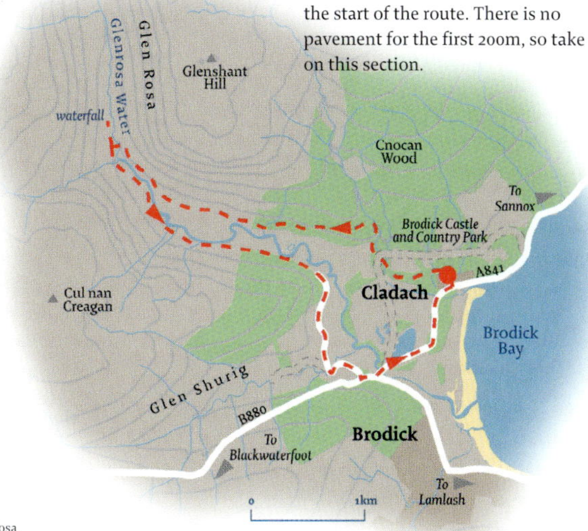


◂ Glen Rosa

# Three Beinns Horseshoe

**Distance 14.5km Time 6 hours 30 Terrain rocky mountain and moorland, generally good paths; Coire a' Bhradain can be very boggy Map OS Explorer 361 Access bus to the start of the minor road to Glen Rosa from Brodick**

**This rewarding route takes in the summits of Beinn Nuis, Beinn Tarsuinn and Beinn a' Chliabhain which form the ridge above Coire a' Bhradain west of Glen Rosa. It is a fairly demanding walk which involves some easy scrambling on the descent from Beinn Tarsuinn.**

Where the Glen Rosa road ends, follow the track beside woodland and go through two gates. The generally firm, dry track winds through the glen, staying close to the Glenrosa Water, with views opening up to Goatfell on the right and the pyramidal peak of Cir Mhòr at the head of the glen. After 2km, cross a footbridge over the Garbh Allt and turn left on a path to soon climb steeply, roughly parallel to the river. Go through a kissing gate and continue uphill between a fence and the river as the gradient eases. Ignore the turning towards Beinn a' Chliabhain on your right, and continue through another gate so fence and river are both on your left. There are good views into Coire a' Bhradain and the horseshoe ridge with Beinn Tarsuinn at its head.

After following the path near the burn, go through a third gate on your left and cross the Garbh Allt on boulder stepping stones. Once across, ignore a stile and continue by the burn until the path along the bank ends; now bear left towards a gate in a deer fence. Go through this and follow the grassy path leading northwest up the southeastern flank of Beinn Nuis.

At around 650m, keep to the right edge of the ridge where paths thread a way

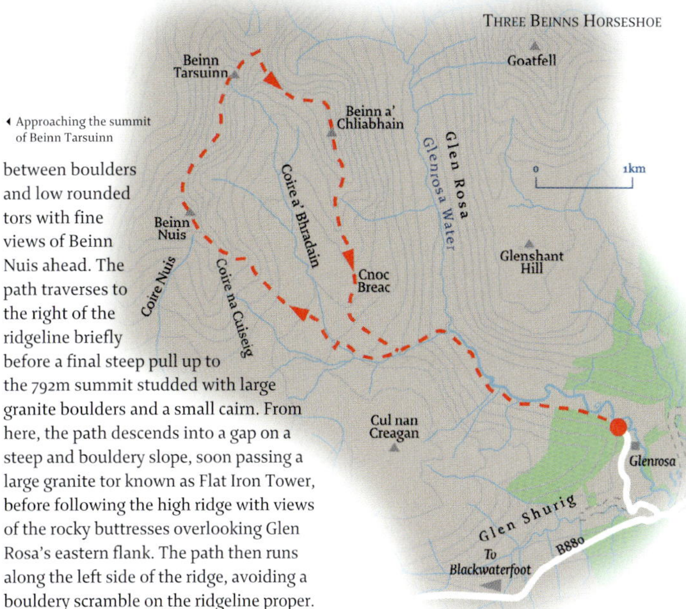


◂ Approaching the summit of Beinn Tarsuinn

between boulders and low rounded tors with fine views of Beinn Nuis ahead. The path traverses to the right of the ridgeline briefly before a final steep pull up to the 792m summit studded with large granite boulders and a small cairn. From here, the path descends into a gap on a steep and bouldery slope, soon passing a large granite tor known as Flat Iron Tower, before following the high ridge with views of the rocky buttresses overlooking Glen Rosa's eastern flank. The path then runs along the left side of the ridge, avoiding a bouldery scramble on the ridgeline proper. Beinn Tarsuinn's summit (826m) is adorned with granite boulders and enjoys panoramic views in all directions.

The steep descent towards the Bealach an Fhir-bhogha follows an intermittent worn path between substantial boulders and granite outcrops, with some scrambling. There are some large steps between easier sections with a few stretches of constructed path. Before you reach the cairn-marked bealach, bear right immediately after Consolation Tor, a distinctive rocky knoll on the ridge. A clear path descends from here to the ridge above Coire Daingean with Beinn a' Chliabhain ahead.

The path keeps to the right side of the ridge at times to avoid some scrambling on the ridgeline. Cross some easy slabs, then before the final climb to the summit keep left where the path forks to stay on the grassy ridge. Some easy scrambling over huge rounded boulders leads to the top of Beinn a' Chliabhain (675m). From the summit, follow the path southwards down the ridge with views across Glen Rosa and Brodick beyond. Go through a deer fence gate and continue down the ridge on often boggy ground. After passing the cairn on Cnoc Breac (401m), the gradient soon eases and the ground becomes even boggier. Go through a kissing gate above the Garbh Allt to rejoin the outward route.

# Glen Cloy and the Fairy Glen

**Distance** 9.75km **Time** 3 hours
**Terrain** good paths, forestry tracks, minor roads and pavement **Map** OS Explorer 361
**Access** Brodick is Arran's bus terminus

**This pleasant and undemanding woodland circuit from Brodick has unexpectedly grand views.**

From Invercloy car park on the seaward side of the A841 heading northbound from Brodick ferry terminal, cross the main road and dogleg right, then left onto Alma Road, which runs obliquely left of the Old Post Office. After around 200m, at a footpath sign for Lamlash, turn right along an unsurfaced lane, climbing gently. At a four-way junction continue straight ahead to climb along a red earth path.

This leads through a tunnel of gorse, deciduous trees and rhododendrons – a Forestry Commission sign indicates the Roots of Arran Community Woodland. Ignore paths signed for the Pond and Orchard to eventually reach a footbridge by a ford at a picturesque convergence of burns. Cross this and continue up the path, soon bearing left over another footbridge.

The path continues climbing to reach a parking area with a view indicator for the vista of Arran's mountains to the north. Follow the path running parallel to the road from the top end of the car park. This soon arrives at the Cnoc na Dail car park and picnic area just across the road from the Bronze Age stone circle, which was also a meeting place for local crofters.

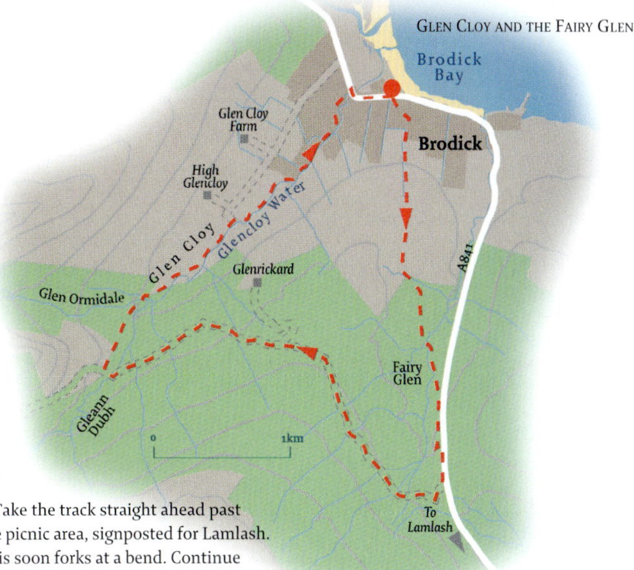


Take the track straight ahead past the picnic area, signposted for Lamlash. This soon forks at a bend. Continue straight ahead (right) here, signposted for Glen Cloy, keeping right of the forestry depot. The broad gravel forestry road contours northwestwards, soon passing a stone quarry, with views of the Goatfell range and Brodick Bay.

The track eventually starts to trend southwestwards and make a gradual descent through mixed forestry with fine views of the waterfalls cascading below Sithein and A' Chruach at the head of Gleann Dubh. A picnic table makes a surprise appearance on the right before the track descends to cross a utilitarian concrete bridge over a tumbling burn. Where the gravel track swings left uphill towards the head of Gleann Dubh, look out for a narrow earth path leading into woodland on the right. Keep following this as conifers give way to deciduous woodland, soon crossing a footbridge and then leaving the woods via a metal gate into a field. Keep dogs on a lead as horses and sheep are pastured here.

Follow the obvious path across the field, exiting via another gate on the far side, and continue straight ahead along a track. Where this curves to the left, fork right onto a path signposted for Brodick into the trees. The path soon runs between a field on the left and the Glencloy Water to the right, finally emerging on a track. Bear right and keep along this, passing the various holiday accommodation of the Auchrannie Resort. On reaching the Auchrannie Road, keep right, then right again at the A841 to return to the start.

◂ The Goatfell range from Glen Cloy

# Clauchlands Point and Dun Fionn

**Distance 5km Time 2 hours**
**Terrain earth and grass paths, minor roads**
**Map OS Explorer 361 Access bus to Lamlash from Brodick**

**This short circular walk along coast and cliffs takes in an Iron Age fort with commanding views, returning through grazing pasture and woods. The route runs very close to an exposed cliff edge, so is not recommended in windy weather.**

Follow the shore road from Lamlash to Clauchlands Farm to reach the parking area at the end of the road. Go through the adjacent gate and follow the path out along the coast on the north shore of Lamlash Bay – look out for common seals basking on boulders near the shore. An interpretation panel on a large boulder explains that the bay is Scotland's first No Take Zone, which precludes any form of commercial or recreational fishing.

Continue towards Clauchlands Point with tiny Hamilton Isle just offshore. As you progress there are views of Holy Isle and the Samye Ling Tibetan Buddhist centre near its northern end. On reaching the point, a small post indicates the Arran Coastal Way continuing along the shore and its alternative inland route bearing left. Turn left along the track a short way, then turn right on a faint path leading up to a wartime observation post looking across to Holy Isle.

Now follow a narrow grassy path through bracken along the top of the cliffs, climbing gently at first. Cross a stile next to an old metal gate and continue along the seaward

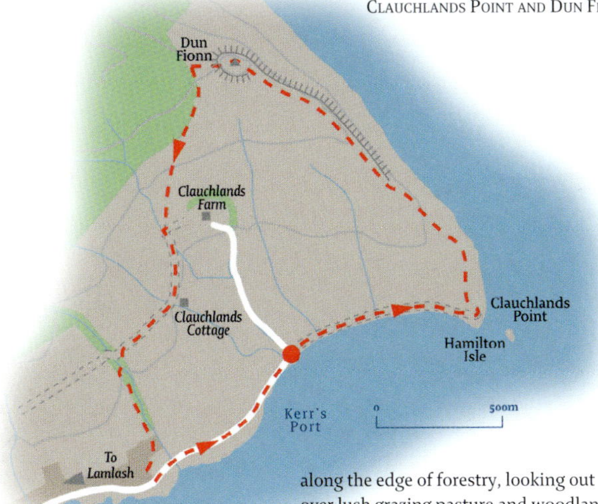


side of a fence and an old drystane dyke enclosing grazing pasture. The space between the fence and the cliff edge is quite tight so stick to the path and proceed with caution. The gradient is agreeably steady and as you gain height there are fine views across to the Ayrshire coast. As you approach the high point of the cliffs, the path climbs more steeply up to the rounded summit of Dun Fionn standing proud from the terminus of the east ridge of the Clauchland Hills with a white trig point. The views sweep from Brodick Bay and the Goatfell range to the north and Lamlash Bay and Holy Isle to the south.

Drop steeply downhill on the landward side of the dun, then climb a little to reach a path junction. A signpost indicates Lamlash along a path to the left; follow the grassy bracken-fringed path downhill along the edge of forestry, looking out over lush grazing pasture and woodland to Lamlash Bay and Holy Isle. Go through a kissing gate and follow a faint path diagonally right down through pasture towards a gate and stile. Cross this and follow the ensuing vague path down across the next field towards another stile next to a house. Cross this and turn right along the farm track.

The road curves left, then heads straight towards Clauchlands Cottage before swinging right, climbing a little and descending towards a wooded area. Look out for a stile on the left (signposted Lamlash). Go over this, follow the path into the trees and cross a burn via a shallow ford. Bear left to follow the path down through the woodland beside the burn, eventually emerging at a surfaced lane by some cottages. Continue down this to reach the shore road. Turn left to return to the car park, or right for Lamlash.

◂ Holy Isle from above Clauchlands Farm

# Clauchland Hills and Corriegills

**Distance** 11km **Time** 3 hours 30
**Terrain** mostly good paths, forestry tracks and minor roads **Map** OS Explorer 361
**Access** Brodick is Arran's bus terminus

**The ridge of low heathery hills south of Brodick is a fine objective for this walk, with panoramic views over Brodick Bay, Lamlash Bay and Holy Isle.**

From the ferry terminal, head up to the main A841 and turn left uphill along it. Take the first left turn for Strathwhillan, looking out for the first in a series of Arran Coastal Way markers. After passing a number of houses, turn right through a gate with a signpost for North Corriegills. Keep to the well-signposted route as it follows fencelines and crosses a series of fields before going through a gate into woodland. Stick to the path as it doglegs left, then right as signposted to emerge on a lane. Turn right before going left along a minor road through Corriegills. The surfaced road ends at Corriegills Bridge; cross the bridge, turn left where a signpost indicates 'South' and follow the rough vehicle track through mixed woodland, contouring around the hillside, then descending a little. Just before the last buildings, look for a narrow signposted track branching right.

Follow this across a small burn, then through dense woodland before emerging on a rough path which climbs through bracken. Ahead, Dun Fionn crowns the steep escarpment at the eastern terminus of the Clauchland Hills' ridge. On gaining the ridge, there are sweeping views across Lamlash Bay and Holy Isle. Dun Fionn Iron Age hillfort is a short detour to the left.

Turn right here and follow a path signposted for Cnoc na Dail car park up along the ridge through bracken, more open areas and mixed plantation. Carry

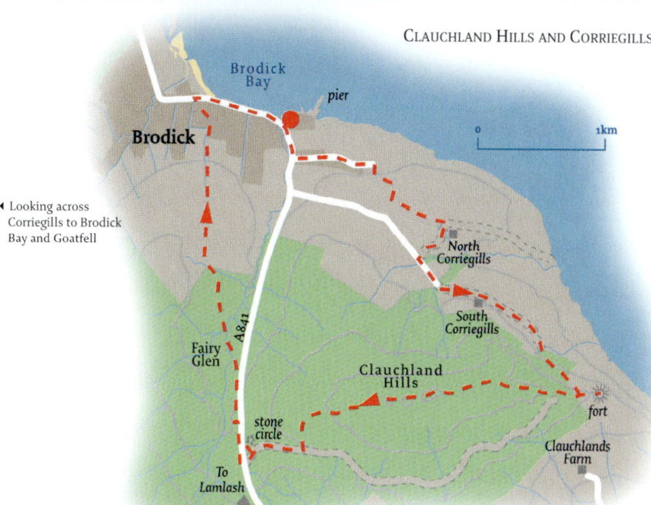


◂ Looking across Corriegills to Brodick Bay and Goatfell

straight on past a large gravel area at the end of a forestry track on the left and keep to the ridge, ignoring all paths off to the right to eventually reach the summit (259m) with its cairn and bench.

Continue along the undulating path through bracken and heather, descending steeply at times and later swinging left towards Lamlash. At a forest road where a signpost indicates 'Circular Route' to the left, turn right, then keep straight ahead at the next junction, again signposted for Cnoc na Dail car park. Cross a low forestry gate and continue towards the car park. Look out for a grassy path branching right for Cnoc na Dail stone circle and fork right again near a picnic table. This Bronze Age monument of four large rounded granite monoliths and several smaller stones was also once a meeting place for local crofters.

Return to the track, continue through the car park and cross the main road with care towards the picnic and parking area on the opposite side. Turn right, signposted for Brodick, along a path running parallel to the road. This soon reaches a small parking area with a view indicator identifying the distant peaks of Arran's northern hills.

Bear left by a carved sign for the Roots of Arran Community Woodland and follow the path down through an area of deciduous woodland known as Fairy Glen. Cross two footbridges and ignore branch paths on either side as the path continues its gentle descent. Go straight over a four-way junction to join a track road and follow this down to a T-junction. Bear left onto Alma Road and follow it down to the A841, turning right along Brodick seafront to return to the ferry terminal.

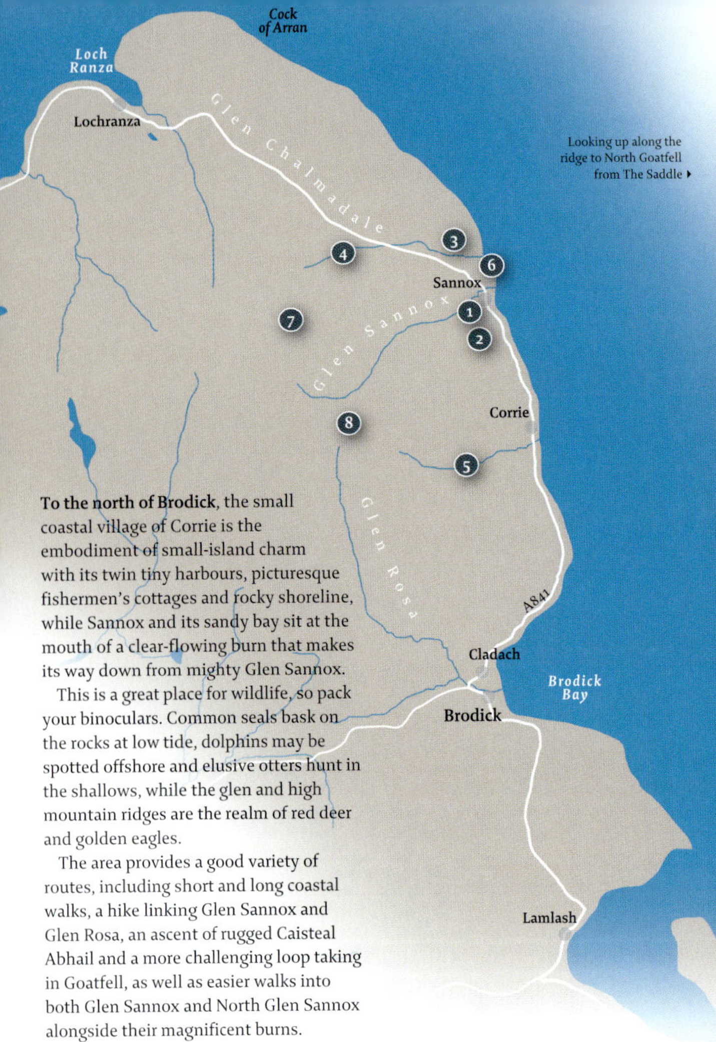


Looking up along the ridge to North Goatfell from The Saddle ▸

**To the north of Brodick**, the small coastal village of Corrie is the embodiment of small-island charm with its twin tiny harbours, picturesque fishermen's cottages and rocky shoreline, while Sannox and its sandy bay sit at the mouth of a clear-flowing burn that makes its way down from mighty Glen Sannox.

This is a great place for wildlife, so pack your binoculars. Common seals bask on the rocks at low tide, dolphins may be spotted offshore and elusive otters hunt in the shallows, while the glen and high mountain ridges are the realm of red deer and golden eagles.

The area provides a good variety of routes, including short and long coastal walks, a hike linking Glen Sannox and Glen Rosa, an ascent of rugged Caisteal Abhail and a more challenging loop taking in Goatfell, as well as easier walks into both Glen Sannox and North Glen Sannox alongside their magnificent burns.

# Sannox, Corrie and the Northern Hills

# Glen Sannox

**Distance 2.5km Time 1 hour**
**Terrain minor road and gravel footpaths, rougher ground higher up the glen; the Sannox Burn is crossed via large stepping stones Map OS Explorer 361**
**Access bus to Sannox Bay from Brodick**

**This short walk loops around the foot of the glacial U-shaped Glen Sannox, which leads into Arran's mountains from the northeast and is separated from better known Glen Rosa at The Saddle between the heads of the glens.**

From the bus stop/car park at Sannox Bay, cross the A841 and head up the surfaced track next to Glen Cottage, signposted for Glen Sannox, going through the kissing gate. The track soon passes the old Sannox churchyard, though nothing remains of St Michael's Chapel that also once stood here. The track becomes an unsurfaced path which swings right, then continues through another gate – dogs must be on a lead as sheep graze on the hill. Two tall navigation masts appear ahead, part of a set that once gauged the speed of vessels in the Firth of Clyde.

As the path makes its gentle ascent, views through the glen open up to the conical peak of Cioch na h-Oighe to the

left, the ridge climbing to the summit of Caisteal Abhail on the right and the spires of Cir Mhòr dominating the head of the glen. Where the path reaches a stand of beech trees, turn right off the main path, signposted for Glen Sannox via the footbridge, and descend to cross this bridge over the Sannox Burn. Turn immediately left on the other side and continue upstream, ignoring other paths striking out across the moor. The path is distinct if rough in places and gives fine views as it follows the course of the river up the glen, soon passing the site of baryte mines that were still working well into the 20th century.

After around 500m, look out for obvious stepping stones crossing the river off the main path. From here, it is possible to continue further up the glen with its splendid mountain scenery or, alternatively, simply retrace your outward route. However, this route crosses the burn and follows the path back on the opposite bank, soon leading to the Allt a' Chapuill a short way from its confluence with the Sannox Burn; crossing should present no problems. Once across, continue past the line of beech trees to return to the start.

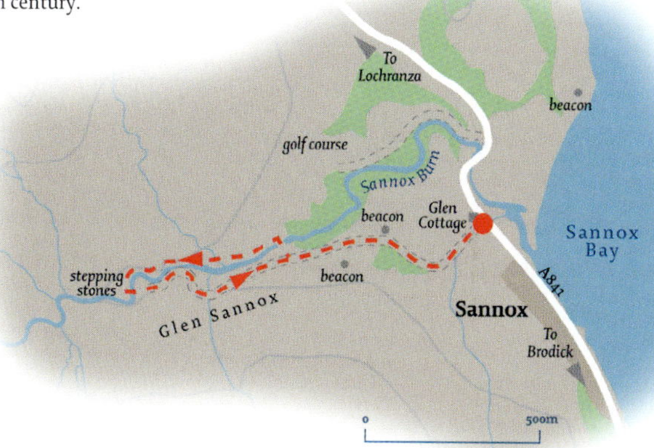


◂ Glen Sannox across the Sannox Burn

# The Devil's Punchbowl

**Distance 6km Time 3 hours**
**Terrain surfaced lane, good path into Glen Sannox; thereafter narrow, often overgrown and boggy but distinct paths**
**Map OS Explorer 361 Access bus to Sannox Bay from Brodick**

**This out-and-back walk follows the wooded course of the Allt a' Chapuill up across moorland and into Coire na Ciche, or The Devil's Punchbowl, the secluded corrie with commanding views below the steep cliffs of Cioch na h-Oighe.**

From the bus stop/car park at Sannox Bay, cross the A841 and head up the surfaced lane next to Glen Cottage, signposted for Glen Sannox, going through a kissing gate and soon passing the old Sannox churchyard. The track becomes an unsurfaced path which swings right, then continues through a gate. A couple of tall navigation masts appear ahead, part of a set once used to gauge the speed of vessels in the Firth of Clyde.

As the path makes its gentle ascent, views through the glen open up to the conical peak of Cioch na h-Oighe rising to the left and the rugged ridge climbing to the summit of Caisteal Abhail on the right. Continue past a stand of beech trees and on into the glen, shortly passing ruined mine workings.

The path soon arrives at the banks of the Allt a' Chapuill near its confluence with the Sannox Burn. Don't cross here; instead

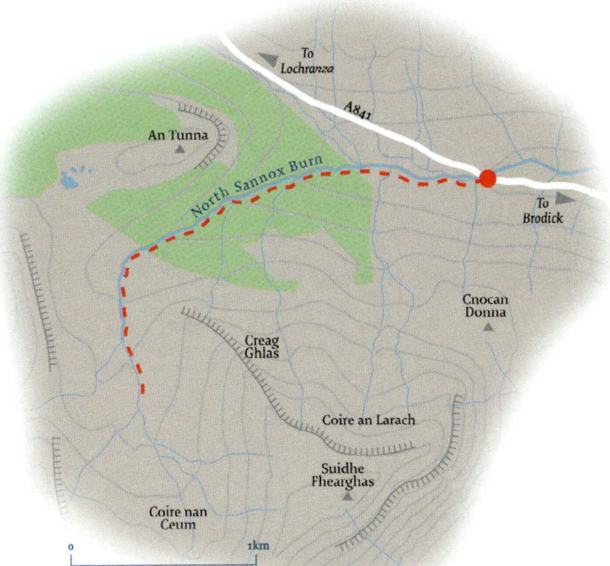


Follow the obvious gravel path leading into the trees from the right-hand side of the car park. Keep left as the path forks by a footbridge (the right-hand fork leads over the bridge to a bench) and continue alongside the burn on the path fringed with heather and bog myrtle.

This soon leads through a gateway, continuing between an area of mixed woodland and the river, and climbing past a series of waterfalls and cascades as the gorge becomes narrower and deeper. At the top edge of the woodland, go through a gateway in an old fence as the path continues upstream, passing more waterfalls. The views now open up ahead with the distinctive cleft of Ceum na Caillich, the Witch's Step, obvious on the dramatic ridgeline that rises to the granite tors crowning Caisteal Abhail.

The maintained path soon runs out and from here the trail is rougher, wetter and rockier. Nonetheless, it's worth continuing for the increasingly dramatic waterfalls and gorges, and the grand views into Coire nan Ceum. The rough path also eventually peters out and at this point it's as well to turn around and retrace your outward route to the start.

◂ North Sannox Burn

# Goatfell from Corrie

Distance **8km** Time **5 hours**
Terrain **mountain terrain, rocky footpaths crossing some very steep ground with scrambling in places; the more difficult scrambling can be bypassed**
Map **OS Explorer 361** Access **bus to Corrie from Brodick**

**As well as taking in the summit of Arran's highest mountain, this exhilarating circuit traverses the tor-studded Stacach ridge and the peak of North Goatfell. It is a much quieter route than the approach from Cladach, although it is better suited to more experienced hillwalkers.**

From the bus stop in Corrie, head south along the A841 for 250m, looking out for a sign indicating Goatfell Summit off to the right. Follow the surfaced lane to a junction, then take the left-hand fork, passing another sign for Goatfell. The lane soon gives way to a metalled track. Follow this until another signpost indicates Goat Fell along a narrower path to the right. The path follows a fence, crosses a small burn, then exits the woodland through a kissing gate.

Continue up the path running above the Corrie Burn with its waterfalls and cascades, soon passing through another kissing gate. The path climbs more steeply, crossing moorland with views opening up as you gain height. The gradient eases as the path reaches Coire Lan with the first views of Goatfell at the southern (left) end of the mighty ridge rising above the corrie. Continue straight ahead up into Coire Lan when a distinct path forks left to cross the Corrie Burn (this is where the return route rejoins the Corrie path).

After 1km the path steepens markedly,

◂ Goatfell from the Stacach ridge

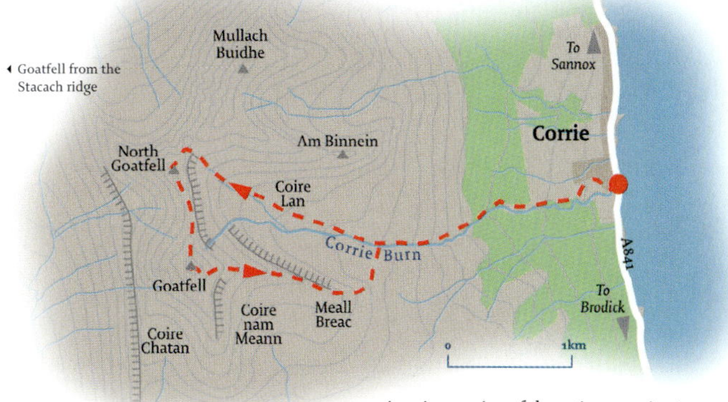


climbing the headwall of the corrie towards the ridge. High in the corrie the path peters out on the eroded slope, but the way ahead remains clear. The ridge is gained at the bealach between Mullach Buidhe (right) and North Goatfell. Turn left with the summit of North Goatfell ahead. There is a little scrambling involved in the ascent and descent, but the summit of North Goatfell can be bypassed by following a path on the east side. Otherwise follow the path steeply up, with some easy scrambling to reach the summit (818m). There are fine views down the ridge to The Saddle with the fearsome-looking peak of Cir Mhòr rising beyond.

There is some trickier scrambling on the descent from the summit, which can be avoided via a path around the west side of the summit, starting high up near where the path climbing up the ridge from The Saddle joins. The path rejoins the ridge just beyond the summit on its south side, then descends steeply to the bealach to the south. From here, the Stacach ridge rises in a series of daunting granite tors. Again, these can be bypassed via a path on the east (left) side of the ridge, leaving keen scramblers to clamber over them.

Beyond the tors, a steady climb through bouldery ground leads to the summit of Goatfell (874m), the highest point on Arran, with its trig point and view indicator. The summit makes for a commanding viewpoint, with Arran's mountain ridges revealed in all their rugged grandeur.

Head down the east ridge, which is bouldery at first but soon joins a good clear path – this will likely be busy with walkers on a fine summer's day. On the shoulder of Meall Breac the main path climbing up from Cladach branches right towards Brodick Bay. To return to Corrie, keep straight ahead (left), following a rougher path along the shoulder. The descent soon steepens, turning northwards before the gradient eases, eventually reaching the Corrie Burn. Cross the burn on stones with care to rejoin the outward route on the far side and turn right to retrace your steps down to Corrie.

# North Sannox coast

**Distance** **3.5km** **Time** **1 hour 30**
**Terrain** **good footpaths and sandy tracks; concrete block stepping stones across the Sannox Burn** **Map** **OS Explorer 361**
**Access** **bus to Sannox Bay from Brodick**

**Stroll along a sandy shore and a lovely stretch of wooded coastline between the outflows of the Sannox Burn and the North Sannox Burn.**

This route starts from a parking area with a bus shelter at Sannox Bay, opposite Glen Cottage and the access track to Glen Sannox. Take the path bearing right at the north end of the car park to cross a series of concrete block stepping stones. Turn right along the wooded path on the far bank and continue alongside the Sannox Burn before turning left along a path parallel to the shore; the path branching right leads out onto the sandy shore of Sannox Bay if you prefer to walk along the beach for a while.

The path passes to the right of a couple of houses as it continues through woodland with the sea shimmering beyond the shoreside trees. At the northernmost point of the curve of Sannox Bay, near a large white navigation mast once used to calculate the top speed of new Clyde-built ships in the Firth of Clyde, the path trends inland. It now continues beneath an unexpected and impressive cliff of conglomerate rock,

before returning to the coast with views across the Firth of Clyde to the Isle of Bute, Little Cumbrae and Great Cumbrae, and the Ayrshire coast.

On reaching the North Sannox Burn, the path turns inland to head along the wooded riverside. A bench provides a good vantage point for watching the river sparkle as it flows over huge water-sculpted sandstone slabs. The path continues alongside the burn a little further before reaching a bridge. If you wish to extend the route, you can cross the bridge to reach the car park at the start of the North Sannox Wood walk. Otherwise, retrace your steps from here.

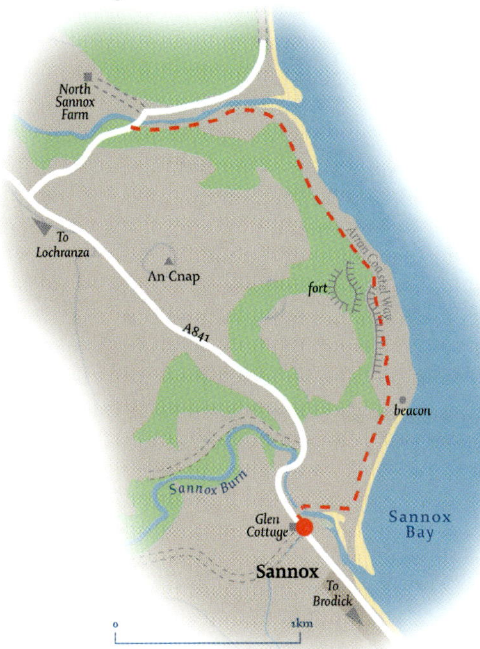


◂ North Sannox shore

# Caisteal Abhail

**Distance** 12km **Time** 5 hours 30
**Terrain** good paths through North Glen Sannox; vague paths lower on the ridge but generally good towards the summit; burn may be impassable in spate
**Map** OS Explorer 361 **Access** bus to North Sannox Bridge from Brodick

**Walk up through beautiful North Glen Sannox alongside tumbling cascades before tackling the exhilarating climb to the summit of Caisteal Abhail, the most northerly peak of the Goatfell range with fine views of the surrounding mountains.**

Take the obvious gravel path from the right-hand side of the car park at North Sannox Bridge, and keep left as it forks by a footbridge. Follow the path alongside the burn, soon passing through a gateway. Continue between an area of mixed woodland and the river, climbing past a series of waterfalls and cascades as the gorge becomes narrower and deeper. At the top edge of the woodland, go through a gateway in a dilapidated fence; the views open up ahead to the distinctive cleft of Ceum na Caillich, the Witch's Step, on the dramatic ridgeline that rises to the granite tors crowning Caisteal Abhail.

The path continues to make its way upstream, but leave it here to cross the burn at the obvious ford, using stones where possible. Do not attempt this if the burn is in spate. Once across, carry on uphill on the initially vague path as it leaves the burn behind to head up across open moorland; the path becomes clearer as it swings left with the east face of Sail

◂ Caisteal Abhail (right) and Cir Mhòr from North Goatfell

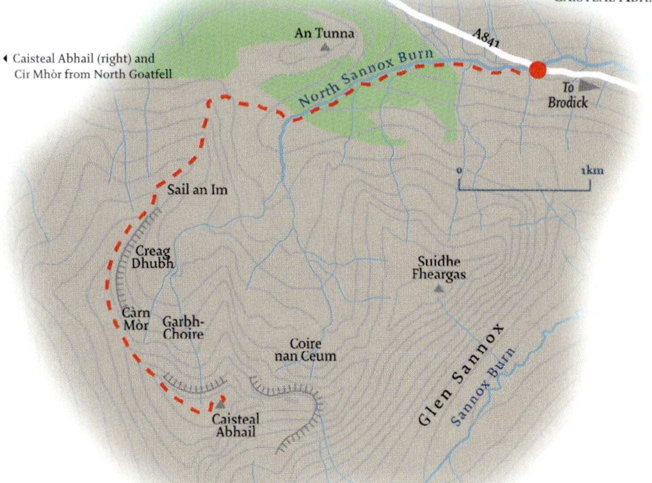


an Im ahead. The gradient steepens as the path weaves through heather, boulders and low granite outcrops before gaining the rounded boulder-scattered summit of Sail an Im (508m).

A narrow path keeps climbing steadily southwest through grass and heather along the rounded ridge to a granite prominence atop the craggy buttress of Creag Dhubh (644m), with a commanding outlook over the Garbh-Choire. Continue climbing along the gradually rising ridge, which levels out on gaining Càrn Mòr (685m) with views towards Caisteal Abhail and northwards back to Lochranza.

The onward path curves left, rising towards Caisteal Abhail as the narrowing ridge steepens once again – the views open up to reveal the A' Chir ridge and Beinn Tarsuinn lying to the south. Bypass a tor to its right before the magnificent spire-like peak of Cir Mhòr is revealed to the southeast. Pass another more substantial tor before Caisteal Abhail's huge castellated and crenellated summit tor comes into view. It presents a formidable prospect, but it is easily bypassed following a path past its left side, enabling an easy scramble to the summit (859m) on its far side. The views are quite astounding, taking in the peaks of Cir Mhòr, Goatfell, Cioch na h-Oighe, Beinn Tarsuinn and their interconnecting rocky ridges. The rest of Arran lies spread out below, between the Firth of Clyde and Kilbrannan Sound, while further afield mainland Ayrshire, Kintyre, Jura and Antrim can all be seen on a clear day. Retrace your outward route to return to the start.

# Glen Sannox and Glen Rosa

**Distance 15.75km Time 5 hours Terrain good glen paths; some easy scrambling to reach The Saddle; minor roads and pavement Map OS Explorer 361 Access bus to Sannox from Brodick to start**

**Catch a bus to Sannox, then walk back to Brodick through the glorious glens that run between Arran's northern mountains.**

This is a popular route with easy walking through the glens, although the climb up to The Saddle between them involves a rocky scramble through the gully of the Whin Dyke.

From the bus stop/car park at Sannox Bay, cross the A841 and head up the lane next to Glen Cottage, signposted for Glen Sannox, going through a kissing gate and soon passing the old Sannox churchyard. The track becomes an unsurfaced path which swings right, then continues through a gate.

As the path makes its gentle ascent, two tall navigation masts appear ahead and views begin to open up to the conical peak of Cioch na h-Oighe on the left, the ridge rising to the summit of Caisteal Abhail on the right and the spires of Cir Mhòr dominating the head of the glen.

By a stand of beech trees, a signpost for Glen Sannox indicates a footbridge to the right. Use this if the burn is in spate; otherwise continue ahead, soon crossing the shallow, rocky Allt a' Chapuill before shortly reaching the Sannox Burn at a ford with boulder stepping stones. Once over, the path running through Glen Sannox is generally firm and well-drained, rising gently at first as you progress towards the head of the glen, surrounded by rugged peaks. Climb towards the low gap in the glen's headwall – this is The Saddle, the crossing point between the two glens. The path fords small burns, then rises increasingly steeply.

Higher up, the path swings right and

◂ Glen Sannox

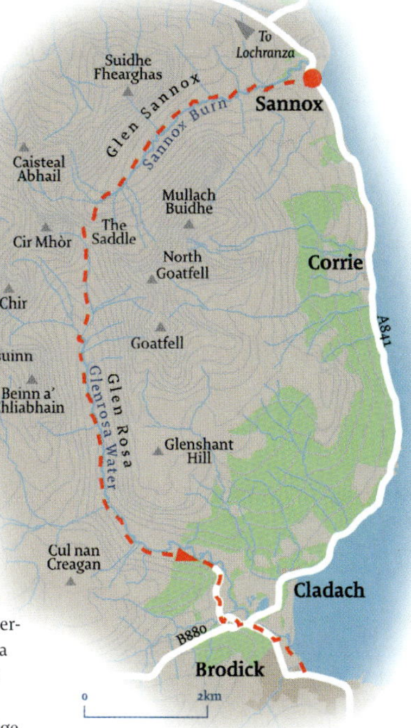


enters a steep, sloping, rocky gully known as the Whin Dyke, an igneous intrusion. The ascent involves some hands-on scrambling and there is some loose material near the top of the steep climb. The path bears left before reaching The Saddle at 432m. This is a realm of rocky outcrops and granite slabs with steep slopes on either side of the gap. To the west is the formidable eastern flank of Cir Mhòr, while to the southeast the ridge rises to North Goatfell.

Cross The Saddle into Glen Rosa on a good path that improves as its downward journey progresses. Keep right of a burn which eventually feeds into the Glenrosa Water, an impressive mountain river. Continue through a deer-fenced woodland enclosure, then pass a series of beautiful cascades and plunge pools. The path moves away from the burn and crosses a substantial footbridge over the Garbh Allt with its tumbling waterfalls. Following the broad track leading out of Glen Rosa, go through a kissing gate in a deer fence, shortly followed by another gate. Pass the Glen Rosa Campsite and follow a narrow minor road past a few houses, crossing a bridge over a burn to reach a junction with The String road.

Turn left along the road, then right at the junction with the main road for Brodick. Walk with care until you join the pavement opposite the Arran Heritage Museum. Continue as far as Brodick Primary School, turn left across the road and take the path adjacent to a parking area. The path soon swings right, passing through a golf course. Go through a gate and continue along the Fisherman's Walk coastal path, crossing a boardwalk, then a couple of footbridges. Follow the path between the shore and a play area, then pass the grocery store to reach the main road again in Brodick.

**Lochranza** is Arran's northernmost village and the island's second, smaller ferry port with sailings across to Kintyre. The picturesque township fringes the shores of Loch Ranza, which is dominated by 13th-century Lochranza Castle standing on a shingle spit jutting into the sea loch. Lochranza is also home to the Isle of Arran Distillery, which sources the exceptionally pure waters running down from Loch na Davie.

Near Arran's northernmost point lies Hutton's Unconformity, a geological feature key to the understanding of the evolution of the Earth's surface over a vast span of time. The neighbouring settlement of Catacol is best known for the Twelve Apostles, a striking row of cottages built to house those displaced from Gleann Diomhan and the surrounding countryside during the Clearances. At the head of magnificent Glen Catacol lies Loch Tanna, Arran's largest and remotest freshwater loch.

Glens, lochs and coastal routes feature among the walks in this area, from short easy outings to full-day and half-day hikes. Outstanding geological features, plenty of wildlife and three of Britain's rarest trees provide added interest for amateur naturalists.

# Lochranza, Catacol and North Arran

# Sannox to Lochranza coastal walk

**Distance 13km Time 5 hours (one way) Terrain good grassy paths to start, rocky and wet underfoot in places, some easy scrambling over boulders at An Scriodan Map OS Explorer 361 Access bus (request stop) to North Sannox Farm road end, 700m from the start**

**Arguably Arran's finest coastal walk, this route runs between steep escarpments and the shore with grand views and lots of historical and geological interest. There's rough walking in places with a potentially tricky bouldery slope to negotiate.**

From the parking area at North Sannox, join the coastal path through a gate in a forestry fence where a signpost indicates the Fallen Rocks. The path makes for easy walking along a raised shore platform as it runs alongside the forest with younger plantation giving way to mature trees. Pass a couple of navigation beacons and follow the track across an outcrop of conglomerate rock. The path weaves a way with relative ease through the Fallen Rocks, a chaotic jumble of huge boulders stretching between cliff and sea.

A narrower path continues beyond the boulders, passing a series of small caves – this stretch can be wet and muddy in places. After Millstone Point, you can see remote Laggan Cottage perched above the shore around 1km ahead, with easy walking all the way there. Laggan Cottage is a great place to take a break, with a fine outlook across the Firth of Clyde to Bute, the Cumbraes and Ayrshire.

The route continues along an obvious

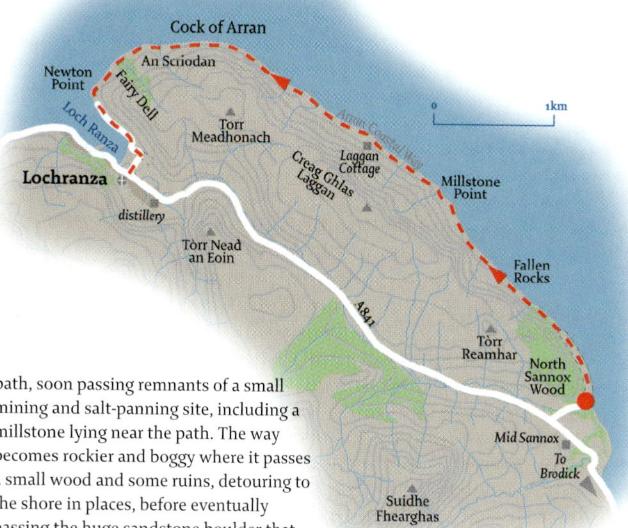


path, soon passing remnants of a small mining and salt-panning site, including a millstone lying near the path. The way becomes rockier and boggy where it passes a small wood and some ruins, detouring to the shore in places, before eventually passing the huge sandstone boulder that gives the Cock of Arran its name.Carry on along a stretch of greensward with remarkable wave-sculpted red sandstone outcrops before the terrain becomes more difficult as you approach a bouldery slope at An Scriodan. Follow the rough path weaving between large conglomerate boulders that came crashing down here in the 18th century. Beyond the boulders is a beach with a signpost pointing back towards Laggan.

The going improves as the path passes in front of a whitewashed little cottage at the foot of the wooded Fairy Dell. Cross a small burn and continue west along the coastal path. Further interesting rock formations can be seen along the shore, including Hutton's Unconformity, a geological feature key to the understanding of the evolution of the Earth's surface over a vast span of time. Follow the level path at the foot of a slope of scattered woodland, bracken and gorse, soon rounding Newton Point.

When the path joins a road by a house, follow it along the shore, passing more houses, to reach the head of Loch Ranza. Continue to the junction with a path signposted for Laggan, turning right here to follow the road to the T-junction where the A841 passes through Lochranza. There is a bus stop at the Isle of Arran Distillery to the left and another a little further away at the ferry slip to the right for the return to the start.

◂ Coastline with millstone at Laggan

# Laggan and the Cock of Arran

**Distance 12km Time 5 hours**
**Terrain minor road, good metalled track; rocky and wet underfoot in places; extensive easy scrambling over boulders**
**Map OS Explorer 361 Access bus to Lochranza from Brodick**

**This fine circuit from Lochranza is one of Arran's classic coastal walks. Climb across moorland for views over the Firth of Clyde before descending to the coast at lonely Laggan Cottage and returning along the shore around the Cock of Arran.**

Take the minor road branching off the A841 opposite St Bride's Church and the Lochranza Centre, signposted for the Cock of Arran and Laggan. Follow the road past a golf course, crossing a bridge and turning right onto an unsurfaced lane at a junction, again signposted for the Cock of Arran and Laggan. The lane leads uphill past houses with views across the glen to Creag a' Chaise and Tòrr Nead an Eoin guarding the entrance to Gleann Easan Biorach. After 1km leave the lane where a grassy path forks left by an interpretation panel, signposted for Laggan. The substantial path is the old route to Cock Farm from Lochranza and begins a rising traverse along the flank of Glen Chalmadale.

Cross a footbridge over the Allt Eadaraidh tumbling through a wooded ravine and continue climbing steadily across the rough, heathery moorland to reach the cairn-marked pass at Bearradh Tom a' Muidhe (263m), with views across the Firth of Clyde to the Ayrshire coast and northeast across the sound to Bute and the Cowal Peninsula.

The onward path begins its descent across the steep escarpment with the ruins of Cock Farm coming into view far below. Now completely depopulated, there were once more than 100 people living in the area of Laggan and Cock Farm. Malcolm Macmillan, the grandfather of Daniel

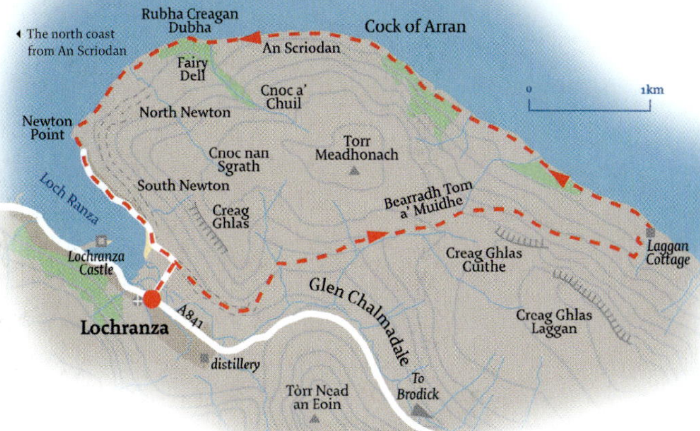


Macmillan who founded the famous Macmillan publishing house, was born at Cock Farm in 1735; his great-great grandson was the mid-20th-century prime minister, Harold Macmillan. Cock Farm was finally deserted in 1912.

Follow the path as it traverses below the crags of Creag Ghlas Laggan before descending more steeply to whitewashed Laggan Cottage perched above the rocky shore. Bear left past the cottage and cross a rocky outcrop. The route continues along an obvious path, soon passing remnants of a small mining and salt-panning site, including a millstone lying near the path. The way becomes rockier and boggy where it passes woodland and some ruins by the shore, before eventually reaching the huge sandstone boulder that gives the Cock of Arran its name. Carry on along a stretch of greensward with remarkable wave-sculpted red sandstone outcrops before the terrain becomes more difficult as you approach a bouldery slope at An Scriodan. Follow the rough path weaving between large conglomerate boulders. Beyond is a beach with a signpost pointing back towards Laggan.

The going improves as the path passes in front of a whitewashed little cottage at the foot of the wooded Fairy Dell. Cross a small burn and continue west along the coastal path. Further interesting rock formations can be seen along the shore, including Hutton's Unconformity, a geological feature key to the understanding of the evolution of the Earth's surface over a vast span of time. Follow the level path at the foot of a slope of scattered woodland, bracken and gorse, soon rounding Newton Point.

When the path joins a road by a house, follow it along the shore, passing more houses to reach the head of Loch Ranza. Continue to the junction with the Laggan path taken earlier and turn right to follow the road back to the T-junction where the A841 passes through Lochranza.

# Fairy Dell

**Distance 6.25km Time 2 hours 30 Terrain minor road, gravel, grass and earth paths, rough track Map OS Explorer 361 Access bus to Lochranza from Brodick**

**Head out around the shore of Loch Ranza and the Newton Point headland to pass a site of great geological significance and a whitewashed little cottage at the foot of the wooded Fairy Dell.**

Take the minor road branching off the A841 opposite St Bride's Church and the Lochranza Centre; a signpost indicates Fairy Dell and Ossian's Cave. Follow the road past a golf course, crossing a bridge and turning left at a junction to follow the road, still signposted for Fairy Dell, passing cottages to the right with a golf course to the left where red deer can often be seen grazing. You soon reach the shingle shoreline at the head of Loch Ranza and the road follows the loch edge past further cottages and a couple of grander houses.

The road ends by a substantial house and turning area; continue along a clear path, passing an information panel explaining the geological significance of the coastline here. The path soon leads to Newton Point where there is a view indicator, then continues around the coast on level ground at the foot of a slope of bracken, gorse and patchy woodland.

An inscribed red sandstone block draws attention to the fascinating geological feature known as Hutton's Unconformity,

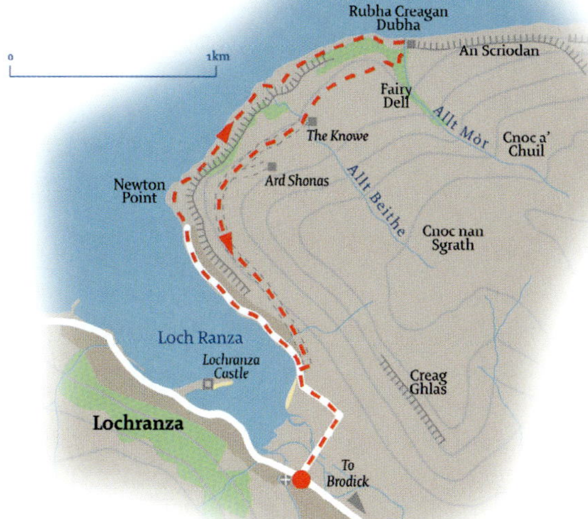


where rocks of vastly different ages join at oblique angles. Ancient schists, a foliated metamorphic rock, are inclined very steeply with younger sandstone bedded almost horizontally on top. These two rock types were formed hundreds of millions of years apart. This is one of the sites where in the 18th-century geologist James Hutton was to develop his theory that the Earth's surface has evolved over an immense period of time. His Theory of the Earth posited that mountains were continually being uplifted and eroded and that rocks were formed both by volcanic action and sedimentary deposits.

Continue around the headland, following the rough path beneath the red sandstone cliffs, then cross a small burn rather unconvincingly named Allt Mòr by a drystane dyke to reach the whitewashed cottage at the foot of the wooded Fairy Dell. Respect the owners' privacy by not approaching too closely. Cross back over the Allt Mòr and turn inland by a dilapidated drystane dyke, following a path into pleasant deciduous woodland alongside the burn. The path soon bears right, climbing out of the woods and passing a bench with views to Kintyre, Bute and Cowal. Continue contouring along the hillside, keeping straight ahead before reaching the end of a rough vehicle track by a couple of houses. Follow this past several houses before eventually heading downhill with fine views across Lochranza, its loch and the hills beyond. The track rejoins the road on the north shore of the loch; retrace the outward route back to the A841.

◂ Cottage by Fairy Dell

# Loch na Davie loop

**Distance** **17km** **Time** **5 hours 30**
**Terrain** **generally rough, bouldery paths beside burns, very boggy in places; quiet road between Catacol and Lochranza**
**Map** **OS Explorer 361** **Access** **bus to Lochranza from Brodick**

**A rough circuit through wild glens and over high passes visits remote Loch na Davie and some of Britain's rarest trees.**

The walk starts near the Isle of Arran Distillery, which was established here in 1995 on the recommendation of Glasgow University's Geology Department because of the particular purity of the water supply from Loch na Davie.

On the southeast side of the distillery, beside Ballarie Bridge, a signpost indicates Gleann Easan Biorach and Loch na Davie. A clear path follows the burn past a pumping station, then begins to rise gently at first before the way becomes steep and stony as it ascends to the mouth of Gleann Easan Biorach. Continue alongside a steep-sided rocky gorge protected by a metal fence. The burn tumbles over waterfalls beneath the flank of Tòrr Nead an Eoin as the gradient eases and the path contours across a broad moorland slope close to the burn.

After traversing frequently boggy ground, the path crosses a couple of tributary burns flowing down the flank of Meall Mòr; the second of these, the Allt Dubh, requires a short scramble up the far side. The path soon begins climbing a boulder-strewn slope to reach a heathery bealach at around 360m. The narrow gap holds the shallow waters of diminutive Loch na Davie – unusually, the lochan has outflows both northwards into Gleann Easan Biorach and south into Glen Iorsa.

Follow the path to the right of the loch, passing a cairn and gradually swinging

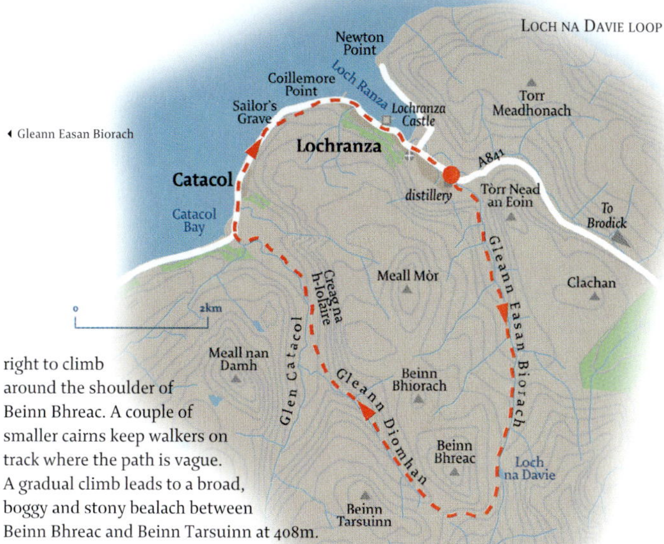


right to climb around the shoulder of Beinn Bhreac. A couple of smaller cairns keep walkers on track where the path is vague. A gradual climb leads to a broad, boggy and stony bealach between Beinn Bhreac and Beinn Tarsuinn at 408m. Begin the descent into Gleann Diomhan on a narrow stony path running parallel to the burn on its eastern side. At length, you reach a deer fence before the burn passes through a granite gorge.

Go through the kissing gate into the Gleann Diomhan National Nature Reserve. The enclosure protects three extremely rare species of tree unique to the Isle of Arran that thrive here: the Arran Whitebeam (*Sorbus arranensis*), the Arran Split-Leaved Whitebeam (*Sorbus pseudofennica*) and the Catacol Whitebeam (*Sorbus pseudomeinichii*). These are essentially whitebeam crossed with rowan, which bear clusters of berries when in fruit.

Exit the enclosure through another kissing gate near the foot of the glen and follow the narrow path down into Glen Catacol. Below, the Abhainn Mòr tumbles over small rapids, waterfalls and slabs of granite with occasional boulders marooned mid-stream. The glen opens out below the craggy escarpment of Creag na h-Iolaire and the path joins the Glen Catacol path at a cairn; carry straight on along the path through the glen beside the burn until its final meanders. Go through a gate in a deer fence before arriving at the road by a concrete roadbridge.

Turn right to follow the road towards Catacol. Pass the terrace of cottages known as the Twelve Apostles and further houses as you continue along the shoreside verge beneath wooded cliffs. After a lone house, bear right onto a grassy track running parallel to the road at the foot of the cliffs. This leads past the Sailor's Grave before rejoining the road for the final stretch back to Lochranza.

# Lochranza and Catacol circular

**Distance 6.5km Time 2 hours 30 Terrain lanes, footpaths, tracks and a quiet minor road Map OS Explorer 361 Access bus to Lochranza from Brodick**

**A circular walk full of historical interest links these neighbouring settlements at Arran's northern end.**

Start the walk with a visit to the impressively located Lochranza Castle standing in splendid isolation on a shingle spit jutting into Loch Ranza. There is a parking area at the shore end of the promontory by the A841.

Lochranza Castle combines a fortified medieval hall-house dating from the 13th century with a later period of building incorporating the castle into a more decorative structure. The original structure was likely built by Dougall MacSween, Lord of Knapdale in Argyll. The building was modernised into the L-plan tower house seen today in the latter part of the 16th century by one of the Montgomery Earls of Eglinton, who had received estates on the Isle of Arran from James II. The Montgomery estates were lost to the Hamiltons in 1705 and the castle was later abandoned, subsequently falling into ruin. The castle was severely damaged during a storm in 1897, but the structure was successfully rebuilt and has weathered the intervening years. Lochranza Castle is now in the care of Historic Scotland.

From the castle, head back to the road and turn right, soon passing the Lochranza Country Inn. Continue towards Coillemore Point, where the Claonaig Ferry departs, but turn left beforehand where a signpost with an Arran Coastal Way marker indicates Catacol up a track leading to several houses. Follow the track as it continues climbing and, at a bend before the final house, bear right onto a

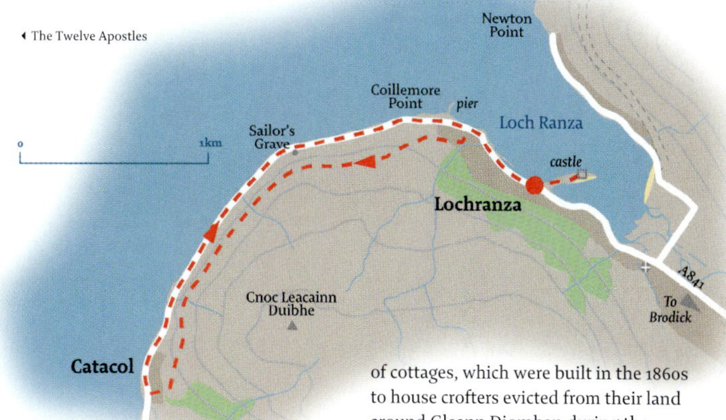


path with an Arran Coastal Way marker. Pass a bench as you follow the path, known locally as the Postman's Walk, uphill, passing to the right of the house and a ruin. At a waymarked junction, bear right and carry on along the path on a boggy slope.

A clear trodden path continues through birch woodland into an open area with bracken and myrtle. Pass dense rhododendron cover, cross a burn and carry on through more woodland to another open area. Cross another couple of small burns, head downhill, then descend several sets of stone steps to a deer gate with a waymarker. Go through and bear right, passing through another gate to reach the coast road at Catacol.

Head north (right) along the quiet road, soon passing the Twelve Apostles terrace of cottages, which were built in the 1860s to house crofters evicted from their land around Gleann Diomhan during the Clearances. However, the crofters refused to live in the cottages and the terrace became known as Hungry Row until other tenants were found. Interestingly, the 12 cottages share 13 chimneys and each cottage has a different shaped upper window, purportedly so that fishermen could see candlelight signals from their families when at sea. Continue along the shoreside verge beneath wooded cliffs.

After passing a lone house, bear right onto a grassy track running parallel to the road at the foot of the cliffs. This leads to the Sailor's Grave – a pile of rocks with a simple stone marker and a faded concrete plaque. John McLean was buried here in 1854 between Catacol and Lochranza for fear of the plague. People passing the grave would add pebbles from the beach to the mound to atone for his exclusion. Rejoin the road and follow it back to Lochranza.

# Meall nan Damh and Lochan a'Mhill

Distance **6km** Time **3 hours 30**
Terrain **faint paths, wet ground, pathless moorland, dense bracken; rocky outcrops**
Map **OS Explorer 361** Access **bus to Catacol from Brodick**

**This initially tough walk over rough and often pathless moorland improves once you gain Meall nan Damh's summit ridge. The route also takes in a hill lochan with tremendous views but is best undertaken in early spring or autumn to avoid the dense bracken cover.**

The walk starts from a small car park near a large house called Fairhaven, immediately south of the bridge over the Abhainn Mòr at Catacol. From the back of the car park, follow the path along the wooded banks of the Abhainn Mòr, continuing through birch woodland to arrive at a deer gate. Go through this, then descend to cross the Allt nan Eireannach with care via some boulders.

The onward path emerges at a meadow near a large wooden hut on the right with deciduous woodland climbing the rugged slopes to its rear. Follow a narrow path through the field in front of the hut, then continue across a wet area with dense heather and bog myrtle. When the trees on the hillside thin out bear right and climb the rough, pathless bouldery slope.

With the summit of Meall nan Leac Sleamhuinn at the top of the slope ahead, bear southwest, keeping the woodland on your right with the heathery slopes of Creagan nan Gobhar on your left. Climb steadily through the bracken and heather using deer paths where you can and aiming for the lightly wooded gorge through which the Allt nan Eireannach flows.

Nearing the burn, look out for a trodden path climbing up alongside the gorge beneath the rocky face of Creagan nan Gobhar, and keep back from the edge of

◂ Meall nan Damh

the gorge. Once above the crags, the vague path crosses wet ground, becoming clearer as it rises steadily alongside the burn. The gradient eases as you approach Lochan a' Mhill, which sits in a shallow depression beneath the domed summit of Meall nan Damh.

Turn right well before the lochan, crossing the burn. Bear left to gain the south ridge and climb southwards up the steep heathery slope. As you gain height, the gradient eases a little and the heather gives way to rocky outcrops and scattered boulders higher up. Shortly after passing a substantial cairn, you reach the larger summit cairn on Meall nan Damh (570m) with its views southeastwards to the high Arran peaks, and northwest to the Paps of Jura beyond Kintyre.

Head back down the ridge and make your way to the outflow of Lochan a' Mhill. To the southeast the jagged peaks of Cir Mhòr and Caisteal Abhail are visible between the whale-backed summits of Beinn Bhreac and Beinn Tarsuinn. Cross the outflow and bear right for a short distance, gently climbing the heather-clad slopes of Meall nan Leac Sleamhuinn to the small summit cairn at 272m. This is a fabulous viewpoint straight across Glen Catacol to the wooded cleft of Gleann Diomhan.

Retrace your steps a short way back towards the lochan before bearing right (northwest) and descending steadily on tussocky ground through the broad declivity between Meall nan Leac Sleamhuinn and Creagan nan Gobhar, trending northwards on the way down. Following animal tracks where you can, cross a small burn and make for the edge of the woodland near the floor of the glen. At the bottom of the descent bear left through bracken and heather with the wooded slopes to your left. Cross the meadow in front of the wooden hut and retrace your steps to the start.

# Loch Tanna

**Distance 13.75km Time 5 hours Terrain rough, rocky paths, very wet and boggy in places Map OS Explorer 361 Access bus to Catacol from Brodick**

**There is magnificent scenery throughout this straightforward though rough, wet and wild waterside route to Arran's largest and remotest freshwater loch.**

A short way south of Catacol there is a parking area on the south side of a roadbridge where the Abhainn Mòr flows out into Catacol Bay, near a large house called Fairhaven.

Cross the bridge and turn right where a signpost indicates Gleann Diomhan and Loch Tanna. Follow a grassy, stony path through gorse alongside the Abhainn Mòr, soon passing an information panel by an enclosure with saplings of rare species of whitebeam endemic to the area. Go through a gate in a deer fence and follow the path initially running alongside a drystane dyke and deer fence with the burn on your right. The path follows the Abhainn Mòr's meanders, then climbs to cross a rocky outcrop where it flows through a narrowing channel below. The path continues through heather, bracken and bog myrtle alongside the burn as it flows over large cobbles and slabs.

A stone pile cairn marks a path branching left to climb gently along the flank of Creag na h-Iolaire, ultimately

leading into Gleann Diomhan; ignore this and continue straight ahead on the Glen Catacol path. Further upstream, as the path passes beneath Meall nan Damh the way becomes rockier, slowing progress; here, the burn runs over rapids and waterfalls, sluicing across slabs of granite. By a second cairn another narrower path branches to the left, climbing up towards a gate in a deer-fenced enclosure in the lower reaches of Gleann Diomhan; keep straight ahead here on the Glen Catacol path. A substantial tributary burn has to be forded via stepping stones before the generally well-defined onward path begins its ascent towards the head of Glen Catacol.

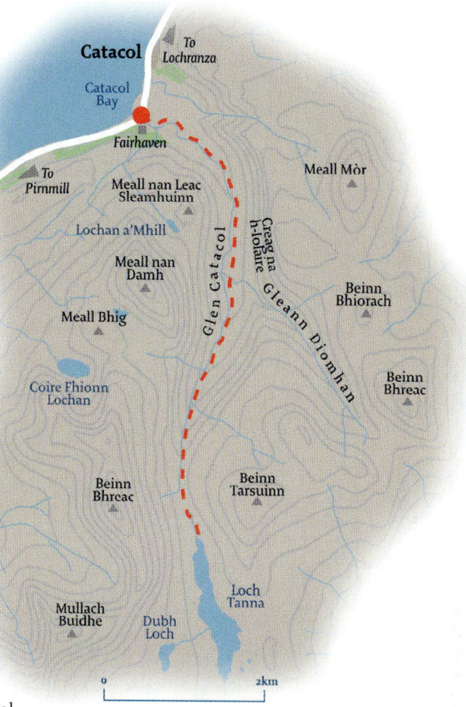

The terrain becomes rockier and boggier in places, passing small waterfalls and cascades as the path progresses, and there are long stretches where the water washes over beds of smooth granite. Walk through a deer-fenced enclosure via kissing gates, passing a clear pool at the foot of the impressive Allt nan Calman waterfall, which more closely resembles a waterslide. Beyond, follow the narrowing burn upstream, passing a stone pile cairn before reaching another large cairn on a broad stony bealach (336m) between the flanks of Beinn Tarsuinn and Beinn Bhreac. Loch Tanna, the largest and remotest loch on Arran, lies ahead.

The bealach is very boggy lower down so it's best to skirt higher up along its left-hand side to reach the loch shore where a cairn marks its northern end. Enjoy the silence and sense of remoteness before retracing your outward route.

◂ Glen Catacol

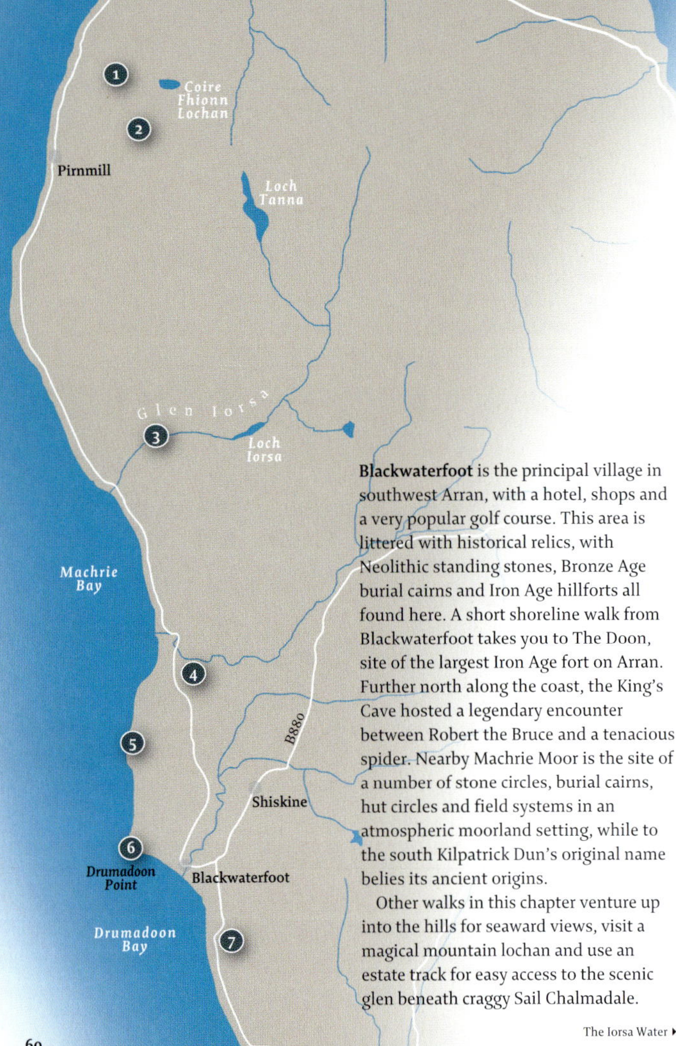


**Blackwaterfoot** is the principal village in southwest Arran, with a hotel, shops and a very popular golf course. This area is littered with historical relics, with Neolithic standing stones, Bronze Age burial cairns and Iron Age hillforts all found here. A short shoreline walk from Blackwaterfoot takes you to The Doon, site of the largest Iron Age fort on Arran. Further north along the coast, the King's Cave hosted a legendary encounter between Robert the Bruce and a tenacious spider. Nearby Machrie Moor is the site of a number of stone circles, burial cairns, hut circles and field systems in an atmospheric moorland setting, while to the south Kilpatrick Dun's original name belies its ancient origins.

Other walks in this chapter venture up into the hills for seaward views, visit a magical mountain lochan and use an estate track for easy access to the scenic glen beneath craggy Sail Chalmadale.

The Iorsa Water ▸

# Around Blackwaterfoot and the west

# Coire Fhionn Lochan

**Distance** 5.5km **Time** 2 hours
**Terrain** grass and gravel footpaths across moorland, rocky in places
**Map** OS Explorer 361 **Access** bus (request stop) to Mid Thundergay from Brodick

**Walk across moorland on good paths to a lovely lochan cradled in a corrie beneath the Pirnmill Hills.**

Thundergay, or Thunderguy as it's known locally, is located off the coast road between Catacol and Pirnmill; there is limited parking by the Allt Mòr bridge. This small settlement was one of a number of farmsteads established along Arran's western side many centuries past. Purportedly the farmsteads' tenant farmers were granted their tenancies by the Scottish kings, including Robert the Bruce, although there is no proof of this.

A signpost indicates Coire Fhionn Lochan along an access road, which climbs before curving to the left. On passing the last house, go through a kissing gate with another signpost for Coire Fhionn Lochan, and follow the path up a bracken-covered slope, soon crossing a deer fence on a ladder stile.

The path becomes clearer as it traverses a heathery slope with the whale-backed summit of Meall nan Damh looming ahead. Cross a burn on large stepping stones, then turn sharply right to continue climbing alongside the Uisge

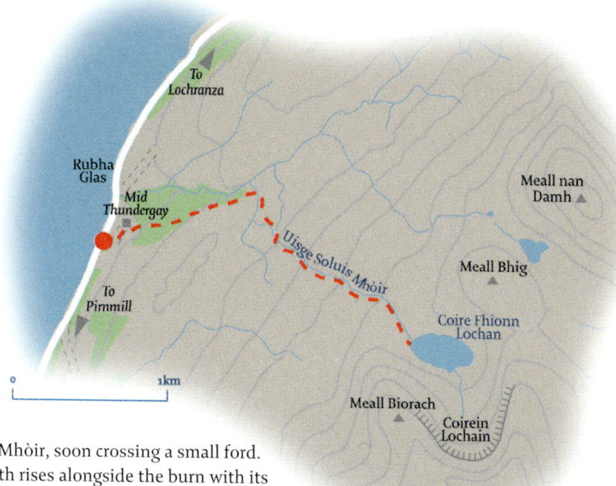


Soluis Mhòir, soon crossing a small ford. The path rises alongside the burn with its series of small waterfalls tumbling down through a narrow gorge where gnarly birch and rowan trees cling to the rocky edges. As height is gained, the onward route climbs a rocky staircase, then crosses a series of granite slabs, which are slippery in wet conditions, while the burn cascades over slabs to the left.

The gradient eases as the well-maintained path progresses towards the corrie, which is ringed by the ridge swinging around from Meall Biorach on the right to the smaller summit of Meall Bhig beyond the bealach to the left. Coire Fhionn Lochan soon comes into view, cradled in the coire beneath the rounded rocky hills. Its name approximately translates as 'little loch of the pale corrie'.

At its outflow is a white sand beach composed of fine granite gravel, a great spot to soak up your surroundings. On a warm day, the clear waters might inspire the adventurous to enjoy a paddle or even a dip before retracing the outward route back to Thundergay.

As you follow the path back down alongside the Uisge Soluis Mhòir, there are expansive views across the Kilbrannan Sound to Kintyre with the distinctive quartzite domes of the Paps of Jura visible beyond the peninsula to the northwest.

◂ Coire Fhionn Lochan

◂ xxxx

# Pirnmill Horseshoe

**Distance 14.5km Time 7 hours**
**Terrain grassy and stony ridges, mostly good paths; some boggy sections**
**Map OS Explorer 361 Access bus to Mid Thundergay from Brodick**

**Stride out across a whale-backed mountain ridge with tremendous views for a long and rewarding day in the hills.**

From the coast road between Catacol and Pirnmill, a sign indicates Coire Fhionn Lochan along an access road, which climbs before curving left. After passing the last house, go through a kissing gate with another signpost. Follow the path up a bracken-covered slope, soon crossing a deer fence on a ladder stile. The path becomes clearer as it traverses a heathery slope with the rounded summit of Meall nan Damh looming ahead. Cross a burn on stepping stones, then turn sharply right to climb alongside the Uisge Soluis Mhòir. The path climbs a rock staircase, then a series of granite slabs with the burn cascading over slabs to the left.

Continue towards the corrie, which is ringed by the ridge swinging around from Meall Biorach on the right to the smaller summit of Meall Bhig beyond the bealach to the left. At around 320m, leave the path and cross the burn. Climb eastwards across pathless boggy ground towards the bealach where a cairn is visible in clear conditions. A path is soon joined and becomes more distinct as it rises, with views of Coire Fhionn Lochan below to the right. On gaining the bealach, turn right by the first large cairn to pick up a path climbing southwards, steeply at first, to a wide bouldery summit marked with a cairn (653m). Follow the narrow path south along the broad ridge, losing a little height before climbing gently to the large cairn on Beinn Bhreac's summit (711m).

Descend steadily southeast, trending south across a slight rise, then southwest

◂ Mullach Buidhe from Beinn Bhreac

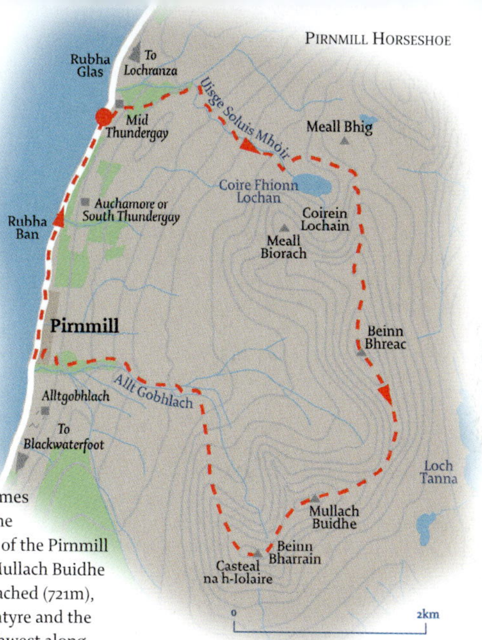

down to the Bealach an Fharaidh at the head of Glas Choirein. There are fine views eastwards to Loch Tanna and across Glen Iorsa to the high mountain ridges of north Arran gathering towards the spire-like summit of Cir Mhòr. Continue southwest along the ridge, trending west across bouldery ground. The path fades as the ascent steepens and the slope becomes grassier. Beinn Bharrain is the collective name for this part of the Pirnmill Hills and its highest point Mullach Buidhe with its trig point is soon reached (721m), with views across Arran, Kintyre and the Paps of Jura. Continue southwest along the ridge, following the path down past granite tors to a bealach before zigzagging steeply up through the granite slabs of a prominent tor. Continue westwards from the tor, following the path across the grassy summit to the cairn marking the southwest top, Casteal na h-Iolaire (717m).

Bear northwest across the summit, making for a small tor. Follow the path down the steepening boulder-scattered spine of the ridge, being careful not to lose it where it crosses some granite slabs. As the gradient eases, the ground becomes boggier and the path vaguer. At the foot of the ridge, head northwest across boggy moorland to cross the Allt Gobhlach just below a small hydro works, before it descends into a steep wooded gorge.

Once over, follow a path along the edge of the gorge and cross another burn running through a gully. Continue to descend, initially alongside the gorge with views of waterfalls, to reach the corner of a deer fence, heading along its left side to cross a ladder stile. Follow the path downhill alongside the fence through birch and oak woodland, crossing more stiles with Arran Access waymarkers. A final stile brings you to a track above Pirnmill; turn left to take this down to the main road where you turn right for Thundergay, 2.5km to the north.

# Glen Iorsa

**Distance 7.5km Time 2 hours 30**
**Terrain surfaced track at the start, grass and gravel footpaths and good unsurfaced track through the glen; two shallow fords**
**Map OS Explorer 361 Access bus to Dougarie from Brodick**

**This undemanding out-and-back walk follows the course of Arran's mightiest burn through a scenic glen to reach the boathouse at the foot of Loch Iorsa. Gaiters are useful when crossing the fords.**

There is no access to Glen Iorsa via the main entrance track for Dougarie Lodge; a well-signposted footpath leads directly away from a lay-by on the coast road, west of the lodge drive and opposite a cottage.

Cross the road from the lay-by to join the surfaced track next to the cottage; a sign indicates Footpath to Loch Iorsa. The track passes between grazing pasture fields, then turns sharply left; leave it here to continue straight ahead (footpath sign) and climb a series of broken stone steps next to a drystane dyke. Cross some awkward large stones at the top of the rise and continue along the obvious grassy path between the dyke and a fence. At the end of the fenceline, a footpath sign directs you straight on. Follow the clear path descending gently through scrub into a small area of deciduous woodland; there are views over the pastureland around Dougarie Lodge below to the right.

The path climbs a little, then descends to meet the main track through the glen at a bend, well beyond Dougarie Lodge at this point. Bear left and cross a shallow concrete ford across the Allt na h' Airighe – this is seldom deep enough to require boots off – and continue along the well-made track parallel to the broad bouldery Iorsa Water. Ignore a footbridge over the burn on the right and continue up the glen with excellent views to distant Beinn Tarsuinn and Beinn Nuis. Go through a gate in a tall deer fence and cross another concrete ford across the Scaftigill Burn; again this is unlikely to require boots off.

Once across, keep following the track alongside the Iorsa Water, which is the widest burn on Arran and one of its two salmon rivers – a series of weirs divide the fishing into 16 pools over two beats. Eventually, you come to the scenically located boathouse at the foot of Loch Iorsa. It is possible to continue on through the glen, but the path which is grassy, wet and boggy peters out after a while. Enjoy the scenery and solitude before retracing your steps to the start.

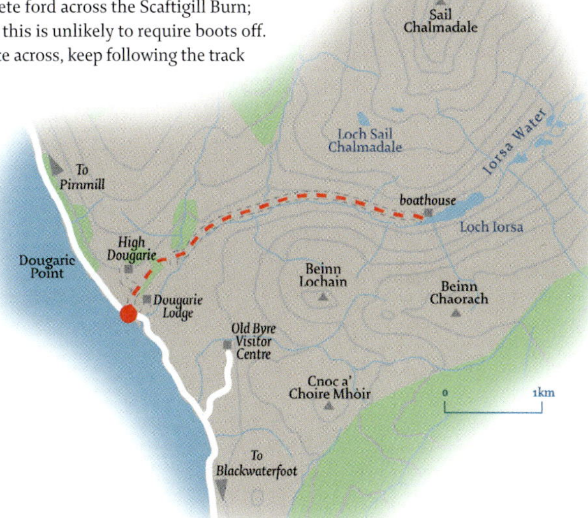


◂ Loch Iorsa

# Machrie Moor

**Distance 4.5km Time 1 hour 30**
**Terrain good track to start, grassy paths and wet moorland around the stones**
**Map OS Explorer 361 Access bus (request stop) to the car park at Tormore near the Machrie Water, 5km north of Blackwaterfoot on the coast road**

**With its impressive standing stones, Machrie Moor is the best known archaeological site on the island. This easy out-and-back walk visits the remarkable remnants of six Neolithic stone circles in their moorland setting against a backdrop of the highest and most rugged of Arran's mountains.**

The walk starts beside the coast road, south of the bridge over the Machrie Water. A sign next to the road indicates Machrie Moor Stone Circle at the entrance to a small parking area. Leave the car park through the gate and follow the obvious track between fields. The track rises gently, then doglegs right and left. At a gate and stile, the Moss Farm Road Cairn stands in a fenced enclosure; there is a detailed information panel here close to the fence so that there is no need to enter the enclosure. The kerbed cairn is the burial site of an important individual who died around 4000 years ago.

Carry on along the track over a gentle moorland rise, soon passing through another gate. The ruins of Moss Farm come into view, along with the double stone circle of Suidhe Coire Fhionn, or Fingal's Cauldron Seat, named after the legendary warrior. Legend has it that Fingal tied his dog Bran to the stone with the hole in the outer circle while he

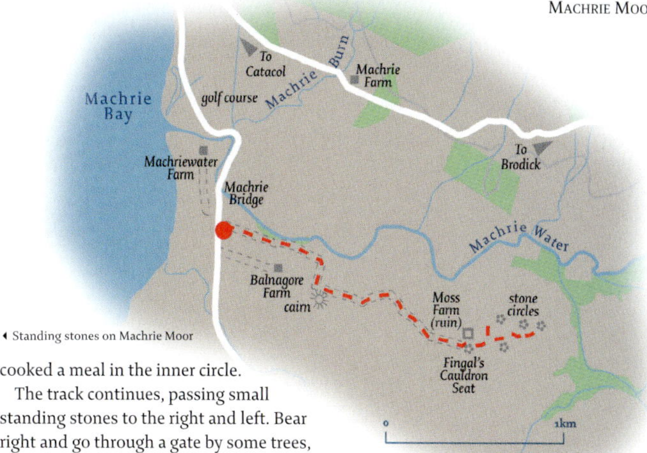


◂ Standing stones on Machrie Moor

cooked a meal in the inner circle.

The track continues, passing small standing stones to the right and left. Bear right and go through a gate by some trees, where there are information panels about Machrie Moor and views to the most impressive standing stones beyond. Further on, there is a small stone circle to the right while a path detours left to a particularly impressive solitary stone. The main path leads to three red sandstone monoliths, the tallest more than 5m high. Beyond are two more stone circles. Lending to the overall atmosphere of the moorland setting is the impressive backdrop, comprising the peaks of Beinn Bharrain, Sail Chalmadale, Beinn Nuis, Goatfell and Àrd Bheinn.

The Machrie Moor stone circles date from the Bronze Age around 1800BC, but archaeological excavations suggest the site was used for ritual purposes far earlier. Around 4500 years ago, in the late Neolithic period, several timber circles were erected on the moor in roughly the same area as the subsequent stone circles. The site later returned to agricultural use before the construction of the stone circles began.

In common with other stone circles, this site likely served an astronomical function relating to the phases of the sun and moon and the changing seasons. Viewed from the southwest, the six stone circles are situated below a prominent notch on the skyline to the northeast where Machrie Glen splits into twin steep-sided glens. The notch is intersected by the rising sun at summer solstice, which likely accounts for the siting of the circles here.

As well as stone circles and standing stones, the area around Machrie Moor is dotted with other prehistoric remains, including burial cairns, cists and numerous hut circles suggesting a settled and long-lived agricultural community. Once you have visited the various stones to your satisfaction, retrace your route along the gravel track to return to the small car park beside the main road.

# The King's Cave

**Distance 6km Time 3 hours**
**Terrain maintained woodland paths, shingle and grassy paths along the shore**
**Map OS Explorer 361 Access bus to car park, 3km north of Blackwaterfoot**

**This enjoyable walk through woodland leads out to the coast and a series of caves in sandstone cliffs, including the King's Cave in which Robert the Bruce is said to have sheltered and encountered an inspirational spider. The route continues briefly along the coast before returning inland through woodland.**

The King's Cave car park is located off the coast road between Blackwaterfoot and Tormore and is announced by a pair of green Forestry Commission signs. Facing the information panels at the rear of the parking area, take the path on the right and follow this along the edge of the woodland. There are soon views across the Kilbrannan Sound to the Kintyre Peninsula and north to the Pirnmill Hills. After 1.25km, the path curves left and continues high above the shore with woodland on the landward side. The path descends at length before dropping down a switchback through a cleft in the rock to a gate; go through this onto the seashore. Continue along the shingle between the sandstone cliffs and the rocky shore.

One of a number of caves found in the cliffs here, the King's Cave is easily identified by the large elaborate metal grille and gate guarding its entrance, intended to protect the Christian and pre-Christian rock carvings within. The gate appears to be routinely left open, allowing access for visitors.

The King's Cave, or Uamh nan Rìgh in Gaelic, is purportedly where Robert the Bruce sought refuge following his defeat in battle against Edward I of England's

◂ The King's Cave

forces in 1306. Here, legend records, he was encouraged by watching a spider's repeated and ultimately successful attempts to build a web in challenging circumstances. He was inspired to continue his campaign against the English and was in the end victorious at the Battle of Bannockburn in 1314. Kilmory Parish records also suggest that the cave was used for church meetings during the 18th century.

Leaving the cave, head through the adjacent tunnel beneath the cliff and continue along the coast, soon climbing to a three-way signpost. The return path is on the left, signed for the car park, but for now follow the sign for Blackwaterfoot, soon joining a sandy path along a grassy raised beach with the cliffs of The Doon ahead. An information panel draws your attention to dinosaur footprints in the cliffs to landward, although the cliffs are very overgrown and not easy to access.

Continue a little further for grand views of The Doon's columnar basalt cliffs, before retracing your steps to the three-way signpost. Turn right for the car park and follow the maintained path as it climbs steadily up the flank of Tor Righ Mòr, eventually re-entering woodland through a gate. Continue climbing steadily before passing to the right of a large lochan as you cross a wooded bealach between Tor Righ Mòr and Tor Righ Beag. The path levels, then descends steadily, eventually drawing close to the road before returning you to the car park.

# Drumadoon and The Doon

**Distance 4km Time 2 hours**
**Terrain sand and shingle beach, paths through a boulderfield and pasture, gravel paths in golf course Map OS Explorer 361**
**Access bus to Blackwaterfoot from Brodick**

**This short and varied circular walk follows the shore northwest of Blackwaterfoot, rounding Drumadoon Point before traversing a boulderfield beneath the spectacular columnar basalt cliffs of The Doon. A gentle return leads through grassy meadows and a golf course.**

The walk starts from the public car park next to the clubhouse of the Shiskine Golf Club at Blackwaterfoot. Drop down to the shore and head along the beach. Cross the outflows of a couple of small burns and look out for the remnants of several igneous dykes. Continue along the sand and shingle shore to reach the rocky headland of Drumadoon Point with its views across the Kilbrannan Sound to the Kintyre Peninsula.

As you continue around the point, The Doon's impressive columnar cliff face dominates the view ahead. Follow a grassy path through rocky outcrops, looking out for a circular view indicator. Where larger rocky outcrops lie ahead, keep an eye out for a path bearing right and follow this to the edge of the golf course. Continue round the edge of the course to go through the obvious gate ahead. Now follow the path towards the boulderfield forming a slope of large blocky rocks beneath the towering basalt cliff.

A path has been fashioned through the boulderfield by removing obstructions and laying flat-faced stones to ease passage. The stone has good grip – it just

requires concentration not to lose the path. A small grassy path is soon joined on the far side of the bouldery slope. Follow this through the bracken to intersect the coastal path from the King's Cave to the north and turn right (Arran Coastal Way marker). The path climbs steeply around the northern end of The Doon, levels out and continues diagonally right through pasture, soon passing through a gateway next to an old iron kissing gate.

Climbing to The Doon's summit plateau for the coastal views offers an additional challenge for the adventurous as it's very overgrown in summer. Look out for a vague path which leads uphill to a gate giving access to the summit plateau, passing through the remains of a rock and earth rampart and wading through a sea of bracken. Enjoy the summit views and look out for the standing stones hiding in the bracken before retracing your steps to the gap in the ramparts and returning to the main grass track.

Continue down this to cross a stile with an Arran Coastal Way marker, then bear left down to a path junction. Turn left and follow the gravel path along the edge of the golf course, eventually bearing right around the clubhouse back to the car park.

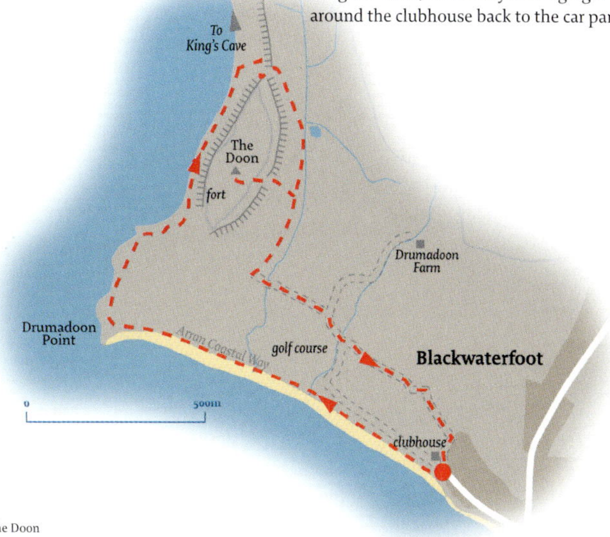


◂ The Doon

# Kilpatrick Dun

**Distance 1.5km Time 1 hour**
**Terrain grassy waymarked paths, often overgrown and very boggy in places**
**Map OS Explorer 361 Access bus to Kilpatrick from Brodick**

**This short linear walk leads to the ruins of an Iron Age dun with commanding views over the surrounding countryside.**

A small walled parking area sits next to the coast road by the entrance drive for Kilpatrick Farm, around 2km south of Blackwaterfoot. The parking area is not signposted hence easy to miss – look out for a green footpath signpost that points down to the coast almost opposite.

From the parking area, walk up the drive towards Kilpatrick Farm, then turn right as indicated by a black and white painted metal post with an arrow. Go through a metal gate and pass directly in front of a house. Continue through another gateway or the adjacent gated stile and climb across a field to another black and white post. Bear left as indicated through often wet, rushy ground, looking out for the next black and white pole by the treeline.

Go through a gate close to the Allt a'Ghoirtean and bear left through boggy ground to climb more steeply uphill onto open moorland. Another pole guides you up to a grassy plateau while the next pole bears an Historic Scotland plaque indicating Kilpatrick Dun.

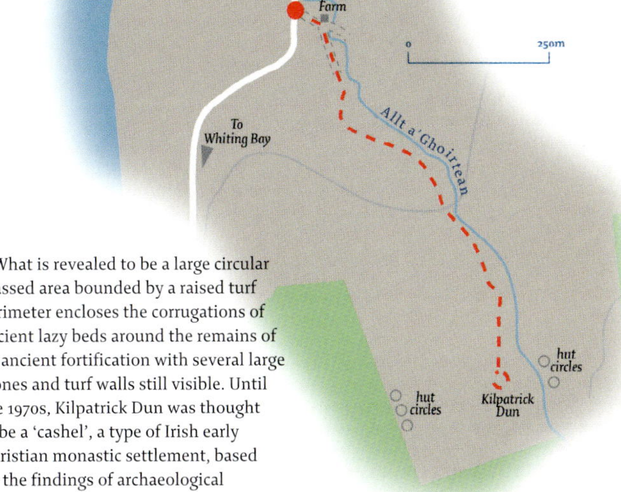


What is revealed to be a large circular grassed area bounded by a raised turf perimeter encloses the corrugations of ancient lazy beds around the remains of an ancient fortification with several large stones and turf walls still visible. Until the 1970s, Kilpatrick Dun was thought to be a 'cashel', a type of Irish early Christian monastic settlement, based on the findings of archaeological excavations in the 1900s. However, subsequent investigations revealed this to be a complex site with several stages of occupation.

The dun itself is a fortified Iron Age farmstead constructed around 1800 years ago and rebuilt as recently as the Middle Ages. A Bronze Age cist or burial cairn was discovered under the Iron Age fort and the surrounding boundary, or cashel, and hut circles are also thought to be Bronze Age. Hence the site is now believed to have been inhabited and farmed since the Bronze Age at least 4500 years ago. The site was referred to as Kilpatrick Cashel for many years and this name is still commonly used.

There are grand views northwards across Blackwaterfoot and the coast to Drumadoon Point and the basalt hump of The Doon. The Mull of Kintyre lies to the southwest with the coast of Northern Ireland visible beyond on a clear day. Retrace your outward route to return to the car park.

◂ Kilpatrick Dun

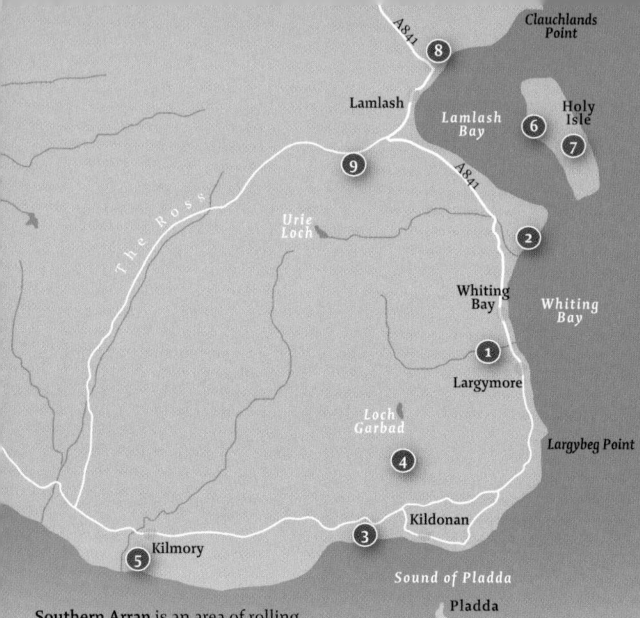


**Southern Arran** is an area of rolling pasture, livestock farms, native woodland and forestry plantation with a shoreline fringed by sand and shingle beaches. Whiting Bay is the largest village and once boasted a substantial steamer pier and attracted well-heeled visitors, some of whom built grand residences. Detached sandstone villas with immaculate gardens are dotted along the seafront road which maintains a well-kept air.

At the southern end of Whiting Bay, a popular walk along the Glenashdale Burn takes in the spectacular Eas a' Chrannaig falls cascading into a wooded gorge and also visits ancient chambered cairns known as the Giants' Graves. At the northern end of the bay a short jaunt to Kingscross Point visits a Viking fort with views across the sound to Holy Isle and north to Lamlash Bay sheltering in its lee. A short boat trip away, Holy Isle is a picture-book Scottish island rising to the rugged summit of Mullach Mòr. It has a long history as a sacred site and was formerly home to the 6th-century hermit, Saint Molaise. A Tibetan Buddhist community has inhabited the island in recent years along with wild Eriskay ponies, Saanen goats and Soay sheep.

Further south, the coastline provides plenty of shoreline walks with wildlife-spotting opportunities and sweeping views across to Ailsa Craig.

Whiting Bay ▸

# Lamlash, Whiting Bay and the south

# Glenashdale Falls

Distance **4.5km** Time **2 hours**
Terrain **metalled track, maintained paths, forestry road; muddy in places**
Map **OS Explorer 361** Access **bus to Whiting Bay from Brodick**

**Climb through a wooded glen next to a tumbling burn to reach a spectacular waterfall and visit an impressive Neolithic burial mound on the return leg.**

The start of the route is indicated by Forestry Commission signs for Glenashdale Falls along the A841 at the southern end of Whiting Bay. There are parking bays on the opposite side of the road either side of where the Glenashdale Burn flows out into the bay. Head along the wooded track alongside the burn, passing several houses along the way. The unsurfaced vehicle track gives way to a good path, although this can be muddy in places. Pass an information panel and continue along the wooded riverside.

At a path junction keep straight ahead, signposted for Glenashdale Falls; the path joining from the left is signposted for the Giants' Graves and this is where the return leg rejoins the riverside path. The path climbs steadily, soon crossing a footbridge and passing another sign for the waterfall before continuing its ascent, quite steeply for a while, towards the head of the glen with the sound of the waterfall coming closer. A wooden viewing platform juts out over the gorge with superb views of the 45m-high falls, known as Eas a' Chrannaig in Gaelic. The upper waterfall cascades onto a broad ledge before tumbling over steps and a sheer drop to the floor of the glen and the Glenashdale Burn.

Continue past another signpost indicating the path for the Giants' Graves on the left – to be returned to shortly. Cross the footbridge immediately above the falls, with a picnic table on the left, for the outlook to the top of the waterfall and the viewing platform across the gorge. A sign warns you not to approach the top of the falls, and the onward route path around the other side of the gorge is off limits due to forestry work.

Return to the sign for the Giants' Graves and bear right to walk up to a junction with a gravel forestry track where a signpost indicates Whiting Bay to the right and the Giants' Graves to the left. Turn left and follow the wide track through the forestry with views out across Whiting Bay to Holy Isle further on. Eventually, you'll see a signpost indicating High Kildonan straight ahead and the Giants' Graves along the path branching left off the track.

Follow the path around to the grass and heather-clad mound in a clearing with an array of unusual upright stones guarding the remains of Neolithic burial chambers which, according to local folklore, once contained the bones of ancient giants. Continue along the path which soon begins its lengthy descent back to the floor of the glen. There are more fine views across the bay to Holy Isle. A significant number of steps carry the path downhill, reminding you of your wise choice to walk the route in this direction. On rejoining the riverside path at the signpost passed earlier, turn right to retrace your steps to the start.

◂ The Giants' Graves

# Kingscross Point from Whiting Bay

Distance **3km** Time **1 hour 30**
Terrain **minor road, rough track, shingle beach, boardwalk, earth and grass paths**
Map **OS Explorer 361** Access **bus (request stop) to Sandbraes by Whiting Bay from Brodick**

**Head out along a shingle beach and wooded paths to a Viking fort with fine views of Holy Isle and Lamlash Bay.**

There is a parking area alongside the playing field at the northern end of Whiting Bay, and the bus will also stop here on request. Walk past the red-brick Gothic church, then bear left at a fork, soon reaching a bridge over a burn. Cross over and turn right (a sign indicates Kingscross to the left) onto an unsurfaced track. Pass several houses and head onto the beach at the end of the track by an Arran Coastal Way marker.

Continue across the shingle, keeping an eye out for a path leaving the beach, signposted for Kingscross Point. Go through the right-hand of two gates and turn right along the path which shortly becomes a series of boardwalks. Carry on through trees and shrubs, soon crossing a large fallen tree by means of steps imaginatively cut over its trunk. Go through another gate and follow the path between a fenced paddock and steep

wooded slope. Further on, ignore the precarious steps leading steeply down to the right, which are unsafe to use.

Emerging from the trees, turn right at a path junction with an Arran Coastal Way marker to cut through bracken and reach a more open grassy area. Continue straight, then turn right with the Arran Coastal Way to the rear of a bench and a rowan tree. The narrow path leads up onto the site of the Viking fort with its few remaining stones, which makes for a great outlook across the sound to the lighthouse at the southern end of Holy Isle and northwest to Lamlash Bay with the Goatfell range rising beyond.

The Viking fort was established on the site of an Iron Age dun, or fortified homestead, built 2000 years earlier. The name Kingscross Point references the claim that Robert the Bruce sailed to the Ayrshire coast from here in February 1307 after his encounter with an inspirational spider in King's Cave and prior to his successful campaign against the English, culminating in victory at the Battle of Bannockburn in 1314. Retrace your outward route to the start.

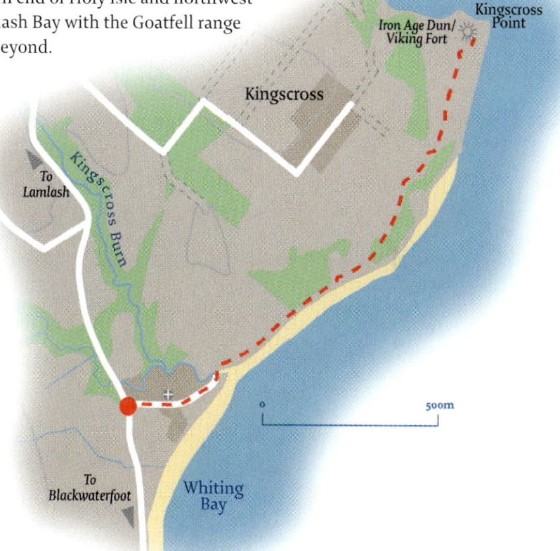


◂ Viking fort at Kingscross Point

# Kildonan shore

Distance **4.5km** Time **2 hours**
Terrain **minor road, track, muddy paths, sand and shingle beaches**
Map **OS Explorer 361** Access **bus to Kildonan from Brodick**

**A short, undemanding out-and-back walk leads along a geologically interesting stretch of coastline with great views and wildlife-spotting opportunities.**

Kildonan is named after the Irish monk Saint Donnán of Eigg, who is believed to have lived here in the early 7th century. He is the patron saint of the Hebridean island where he was martyred along with many of his followers – between 52 and 150 according to competing accounts – either by a band of robbers or a vengeful Pictish queen. Donnán's remains are reputedly buried here in Kildonan.

The route crosses pasture where cows with calves are grazed, hence this is a far from ideal walk for dogs.

This walk starts from a small parking area next to a bus stop along the shore road at the western end of Kildonan, situated between a small green with benches looking out to Pladda and Ailsa Craig beyond and a rocky outcrop which is, in fact, an igneous dyke. Head west (left) along the road, soon passing a war memorial plaque fixed to the rock. Where the main road bends sharply right inland, take the track road branching left to pass several houses and continue through a gate with an Arran Coastal Way marker and a sign indicating a 'common seal haul out zone' ahead.

An interpretation panel describes the wildlife found in the area and outlines other walks along the coast. Follow the path or continue along the shore, soon passing through another gateway with an Arran Coastal Way marker. A number of igneous dykes traverse the shore before striking out into the depths. On a small promontory another interpretation panel describes the formation of the Kildonan Dykes from magma forced up through the Earth's crust during a period of intense volcanic activity around 60 million years ago. The molten lava cooled to form basalt, a dense, durable volcanic rock. The subsequent erosion of the less-resistant surrounding rock has left these igneous intrusions exposed as natural walls, or dykes.

Further on, a series of large flat-faced stones pave a way across boggy ground just above the shore. Dense shrubbery ahead diverts you down across a sandy beach before rejoining the path above the shore. Cross a culverted burn, then look right to the sandstone cliffs where a fine waterfall cascades through an eroded breach in the layered rock. It's worth detouring to the foot of the waterfall for a closer view, but the path is often muddy and slippery as you approach.

Continuing along the shore, pass a signpost for Auchenhew pointing inland along a path and, later, an area of large boulders just offshore that are popular haul-outs for basking common seals – avoid approaching too closely. The small island of Pladda with its lighthouse is around 2km to the southeast while Ailsa Craig with its huge colony of gannets is directly south at a distance of some 20km.

Beyond the next gateway, the onward route is often muddy and then reaches the boulderfield at Struey Rocks; the going is difficult so it's as well to turn around here. Retrace your outward route to the car park.

◂ Kildonan shore

# Eas Mòr and Loch Garbad

Distance **5.5km** Time **2 hours**
Terrain **maintained gravel paths as far as Eas Mòr, narrow earth paths and forestry track to Loch Garbad** Map **OS Explorer 361**
Access **bus to Kildonan from Brodick**

**Climb through woodland alongside a wide gorge into which the dramatic Eas Mòr waterfall cascades, before striking out across an expanse of once dense plantation forestry to reach a tranquil loch encircled by coniferous woodland.**

By the road junction on the inland side of the main coastal road, opposite the road down to Kildonan, there is a public car park next to the Eas Mòr café, and another on the opposite side of the road. The bus will stop here on request. From the car park, follow the path past the café, which initially climbs gently. The path continues above a steep-sided gorge as the ascent becomes steeper, passing several viewing platforms, which aren't of much use owing to the dense forestry. However, the final platform before the head of the gorge provides a dramatic view of the Eas Mòr waterfall plunging over the precipice into the wooded depths below.

Just before the bridge over the Allt Mòr burn running out to the waterfall, a narrow earth path turns left off the main path, signposted for Loch Garbad.

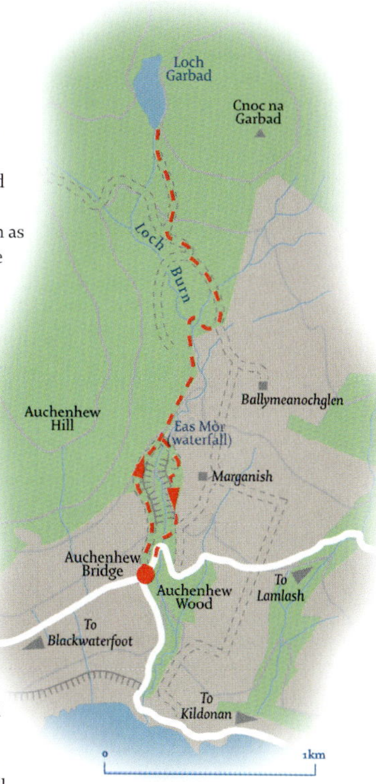


Continue through an area of cleared forestry plantation which is gradually being reclaimed by nature. The path swings right and passes a gate and stile on the right leading down to Ballymeanochglen and the farm beyond – ignore this and continue left.

Follow the path alongside a small burn as you continue climbing gently. Where the path intersects a metalled forestry track, turn right at an Arran Angling Association sign and follow the track for a short way before another marker post on the right indicates the resumption of the earth path. Continue climbing steadily along the path to reach the outflow of Loch Garbad. A picnic bench invites a pause – the freshwater loch encircled by coniferous woodland has a somewhat Nordic ambience.

Retrace your outward route as far as the path junction by the waterfall, then cross the bridge. A little further on, take a signposted right turn to visit the Eas Mòr Ecology library, a large turf-roofed timber hut built from trees felled after a severe storm in 1998, which is extensively decorated with illustrations and philosophical musings on ecological themes left by visitors.

Returning to the main path, you can either walk back to the car park the way you came or for variety continue on the path down through the woodland on this side of the gorge. Just before the old stone bridge carrying the road over the burn, turn right where a signpost indicates the path continuing over a footbridge. Once across the burn, follow the path zigzagging uphill before turning left at a junction to arrive back at the car park.

◂ Eas Mòr woodland

# Kilmory beach circular

**Distance 2.5km Time 1 hour**
**Terrain woodland path, sandy beach, metalled track Map OS Explorer 361**
**Access bus to Kilmory from Brodick**

**This short circular walk goes through deciduous woodland above the Torrylinn Water, then follows a drystane dyke to an impressive ancient burial cairn before descending to the sandy Kilmory shore.**

The walk starts from the parking area at Kilmory Public Hall in Lagg at the western side of Kilmory. A signpost indicates the path to Torrylin Cairn; follow this past the hall and into the wooded glen of the Torrylinn Water. The path descends gently through the deciduous woodland, keeping straight ahead where a path intersects from the right, before soon running alongside a drystane dyke. A wooden gate in the dyke gives access to a well-maintained burial cairn with an interpretation panel.

Torrylin is a Neolithic long cairn of Clyde type built to a pattern found across Argyll and southwest Scotland. When the cairn was built it would have comprised a large rectangular mound kerbed with stones. At one end, the cairn would have had an elliptical forecourt with a façade of large upright stones framing the entrance to a rectangular burial chamber. It is thought the paved area of the forecourt would have been used for burial rituals.

Torrylin Cairn was significantly damaged and reduced in size by later ploughing, stone robbing and dumping of field clearance stones, leaving a roughly circular mound with several exposed stones from the burial chamber. The burial chamber was excavated in 1900 and the remains of several adults, one child and an infant were exhumed.

Continuing, the path soon arrives at a switchback between wooden fences, serving a similar function to a kissing gate.

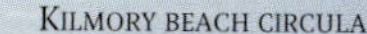

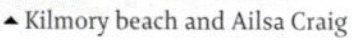

▲ Kilmory beach and Ailsa Craig

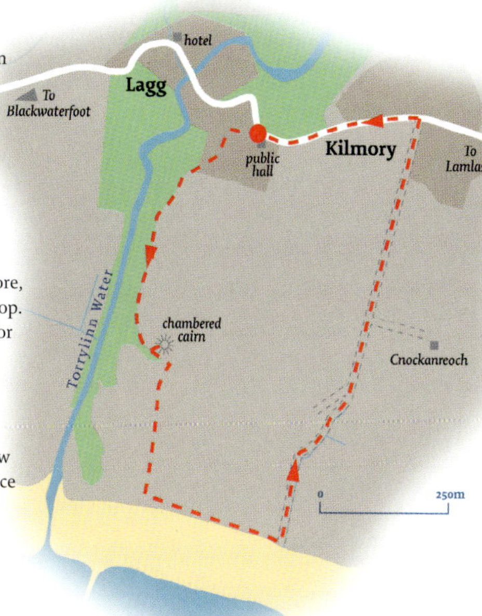


Pass through this and follow the grassy path down through the field towards the shore. Go through a gate to reach the sand and shingle beach.

As always on the south coast of Arran, the granite monolith of Ailsa Craig dominates the horizon. Continue east along the shore, soon reaching a rocky outcrop. Turn left here, signposted for Lagg, and follow the track returning inland.

Turn left immediately before reaching the main coast road to follow a narrow path running between a fence and often overgrown hedgerow parallel to the road, soon arriving back at Kilmory Public Hall.

# Holy Isle lighthouse walk

**Distance 7km Time 2 hours 30**
**Terrain good grassy footpaths on largely level terrain Map OS Explorer 361**
**Access bus to Lamlash from Brodick; passenger ferry from Lamlash Pier**

**This undemanding walk along Holy Isle's west coast is full of interest, taking in a saint's hermitage, a sacred well, a series of spectacular Buddhist rock paintings and the striking Pillar Rock Lighthouse.**

The small passenger ferry crosses regularly from Lamlash in the summer months subject to tide, weather and demand, and less frequently during spring and autumn. The crossing takes around 15 minutes; advance booking is recommended.

Holy Isle is around 3km long and 1km wide and rises up to the rocky summit of Mullach Mòr at 314m. The island is owned by the Samye Ling Buddhist community, and the Centre for World Peace and Health, founded by Lama Yeshe Losal Rinpoche, is located here. On arrival, visitors are generally given a talk by the ferry person or a community volunteer about the island, walking options and a few rules to observe.

From the jetty, turn right and pass in front of the retreat centre where a series of eight stupas depict important aspects of Tibetan Buddhist teaching. Although there is no public access to the Centre for World Peace and Health, part of the adjacent Mandala Garden is open to visitors. Just beyond, The Boathouse provides shelter and information, and

basic refreshments are sometimes available; there are also toilets nearby.

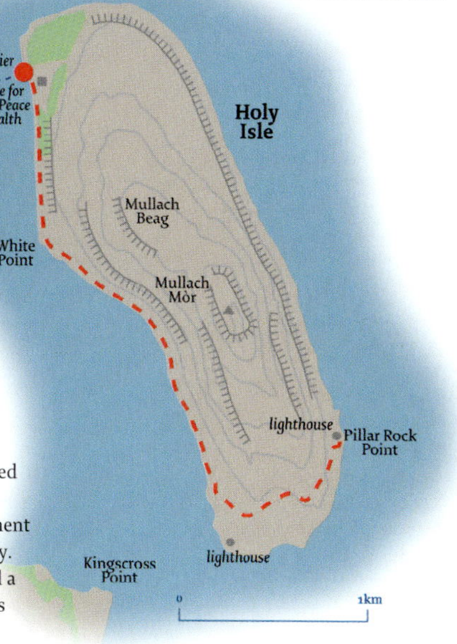

Carry on along the grassy path heading south along the coast. The path is obvious and follows a line of telegraph poles carrying electricity between the island's outposts. After 1.5km a sign indicates steps on the left climbing to a cave at the foot of a cliff, once inhabited by St Molaise, Arran's most notable saint who lived as a hermit here for several years during the 6th century. His Judgement Rock and Healing Spring are nearby. Look out for some Norse runes and a cross etched into the roof and walls of the cave.

Continue southwards along the pleasant path with views across the sound to Whiting Bay. Look out for a series of splendid rock paintings on the landward side of the path; these were created by an artist named Dechi Wangmo, working to a series of traditional designs depicting important Tibetan Buddhist figures. A prominent rock also bears the Tibetan script for the Buddhist mantra, Om Mani Padme Hum.

Approaching the southern tip of Holy Isle, the lighthouse ahead facing Kingscross Point across the sound is known locally as Wee Donald. The lighthouse buildings are home to a community of nuns undertaking retreats and there is no access for visitors. Keep to the path as it slopes up away from the coast, following a fence for a while before continuing straight ahead on a clear grassy path through the heather, with the Lama's Arran residence to the left on the hillside and turf-roofed cabins used for retreats nearby. The south of the island is also frequented by the island's small herd of Eriskay ponies.

Continue to the end of the path at the striking Pillar Rock Lighthouse, which was the first square lighthouse built by the famous Stevenson lighthouse-building dynasty. There is no access beyond Pillar Rock so retrace your outward route to return to the jetty.

◂ Eriskay ponies on Holy Isle

# Mullach Mòr on Holy Isle

**Distance 7.5km Time 3 hours 30 Terrain rough hill path, easy scrambling below the summit; steep rocky path on the initial descent; good clear paths for the coastal return Map OS Explorer 361 Access bus to Lamlash from Brodick; passenger ferry from Lamlash Pier**

**The highest point on Holy Isle in Lamlash Bay is reached by a rugged hill path, with a fascinating return along the shore.**

The small passenger ferry crosses regularly from Lamlash in summer subject to tide, weather and demand, and less frequently during spring and autumn. Advance booking is recommended.

Holy Isle is around 3km long and 1km wide and rises up to the rocky summit of Mullach Mòr at 314m. The island is owned by the Samyé Ling Buddhist community, and the Centre for World Peace and Health, founded by Lama Yeshe Losal Rinpoche, is located here. On arrival, visitors are generally given a talk by the ferry person or a community volunteer about the island, walking options and a few rules to observe.

From the jetty, bear left across the foreshore and pass a four-way fingerpost indicating Mullach Mòr straight ahead, keeping to the left of the Centre for World Peace and Health to head up a grassy slope, following a fence beside a plantation. Make for a gap in a drystane dyke, then follow the path winding up through native woodland. Higher up, the trees give way to open moorland, with a small sign directing you 'To the Top'.

The path is reasonably distinct as it winds its way uphill and becomes clearer higher up as grass and bracken give way to heather. The narrow moorland path climbs fairly steeply, weaving through rocky outcrops as it approaches the cairn-

◂ Summit of Mullach Mòr

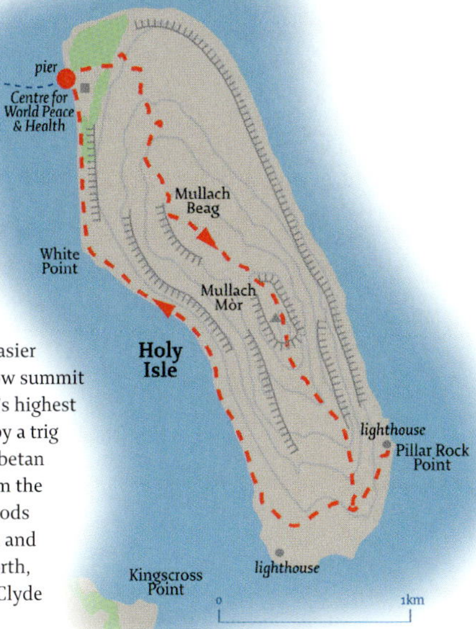

marked top of Mullach Beag at 246m with fine views over Lamlash and Whiting Bay to the south. The onward path makes a short descent to a gap before rising steeply once more, requiring some easy scrambling through the rugged terrain with plenty of good hand holds. An easier stretch of path leads to the narrow summit ridge of Mullach Mòr, the island's highest point at 314m, which is marked by a trig point and often adorned with Tibetan Buddhist prayer flags. Views from the top encompass Holy Isle, the woods and moorland of southern Arran and the mountains of the island's north, a sizeable stretch of the Firth of Clyde and Ailsa Craig.

The path descends roughly southwards, requiring care where it drops steeply through worn, broken rock with cliffs on either side. Where the gradient eases, ropes keep walkers to the path to avoid deep narrow fissures in the rock. Further down, a rounded heathery ridge leads to a clear grassy path running along the line of telegraph poles. Turn left here at the small sign to visit the square Pillar Rock Lighthouse, the first of its kind built by the 'Lighthouse Stevensons'. Return to the path junction and head southwestwards towards the lighthouse, known locally as Wee Donald, facing Arran across the sound. The buildings are home to a community of nuns undertaking retreats and there is no public access. The south of the island is also frequented by a small herd of Eriskay ponies.

The grassy path bears northwestwards, following the western shoreline and soon passing a series of spectacular Buddhist paintings on rocks to the right. The path becomes a little rougher where it rounds a bay fringed by a few trees. A sign indicates steps on the right climbing to a cave at the foot of a cliff, once inhabited by St Molaise. The path improves again as it turns White Point, continuing along the shore to reach The Boathouse, an information centre staffed by volunteers where you can shelter while you wait for the return ferry.

# Brodick to Lamlash

**Distance 14km Time 5 hours**
**Terrain mostly good paths, and minor roads; coast beyond Corriegills Point can be wet and may briefly flood at high tide**
**Map OS Explorer 361 Access Brodick is Arran's bus terminus**

**Follow the impressive coast from Arran's main village, rounding Clauchlands Point to reach neighbouring Lamlash and its bay sheltering in the lee of Holy Island.**

From the ferry terminal, head up to the main A841 and turn left uphill along it. Take the first left-hand turn, signposted for Strathwhillan, looking out for the first in a series of Arran Coastal Way markers. After passing a number of houses, turn right through a gate with a signpost for North Corriegills. Keep to the well-signposted route as it follows fencelines and crosses a series of fields before going through a gate into woodland. Stick to the path as it doglegs left, then right as signposted to emerge on a lane with a signpost indicating Dhunan. Turn left down the lane, which eventually leads past some houses and bears right to continue parallel to the shore before running out by a final house. A signpost (Arran Coastal Way marker) indicates Lamlash straight ahead along the shore where a vague path runs between the high water mark and woodland.

As the path progresses along the coast, the ground can be wet, although there are plenty of stepping stones along the way. After crossing a substantial stile the path becomes clearer, continuing beneath the steepening cliffs rising up towards Dun Fionn. Stepping stones aid passage through another boggy section before the way ahead becomes drier as the path

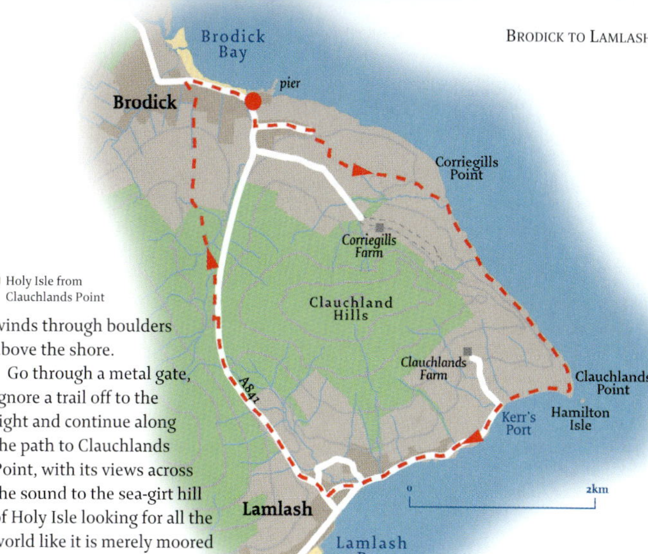


◂ Holy Isle from Clauchlands Point

winds through boulders above the shore.

Go through a metal gate, ignore a trail off to the right and continue along the path to Clauchlands Point, with its views across the sound to the sea-girt hill of Holy Isle looking for all the world like it is merely moored in Lamlash Bay and might set sail at any moment.

Follow the track as it continues southwest along the north shore of the bay, looking out for common seals basking on boulders in the shallows. After 1km, go through a gate and continue along the shore road, soon passing the outdoor centre. In another 1.25km, cross a stone bridge, then immediately turn right opposite a shoreside green and continue along the aptly named Bungalow Road to a T-junction with the A841. Cross to a pavement on the far side and follow this uphill until it runs out opposite the Lamlash Golf Club. A signpost for Brodick on the left indicates a path running parallel to the road. The path soon crosses a footbridge, then moves away from the road into woodland.

Cross the entrance to a small car park and picnic area at the top of the road and continue straight ahead, signposted for Brodick, on a path running parallel to the road. This soon arrives at a small parking area with a view indicator identifying Arran's distant northern peaks.

Bear left by a sign for the Roots of Arran Community Woodland and follow the path down through an area of deciduous woodland known as Fairy Glen. Cross two footbridges and ignore branch paths on either side as the path continues its gentle descent. Go straight over a four-way junction to join a track road which leads down to a T-junction. Bear left onto Alma Road to shortly meet the A841. Turn right along Brodick seafront to return to the ferry terminal.

# Meallach's Grave

Distance **2.75km** Time **1 hour 30**
Terrain **good waymarked woodland paths and tracks; a rougher path climbs to Meallach's Grave** Map **OS Explorer 361**
Access **bus to Lamlash from Brodick**

**A pleasant waymarked woodland walk leads to a Neolithic tomb and the ruins of the cleared township of Lagaville.**

The walk begins from the Forestry Commission car park at Dyemill, on The Ross road heading inland, 1km west of Lamlash Bay. From the parking area, turn right along the entrance track and cross a bridge over the Monamore Burn. Turn immediately right (marker post) to follow a footpath through woodland, which soon leads to a footbridge over the Allt Lagriehesk. Cross this and follow the path signposted for Urie Loch alongside the burn for 500m until it reaches a fork. Turn left – the right branch is the old path to Urie Loch – and cross another footbridge overlooking a small waterfall.

Keep right at a fork (there is a footbridge just beyond the left fork) and follow the path for a sustained climb, later swinging right to pass around a small lochan in a clearing with a bench on the far side. Follow the onward path beyond; on the slope to the right of the path, look out for

a marker indicating Lagaville Village, with only the overgrown mossy stones of a few tumbled walls remaining.

Lagaville was a poor clachan inhabited until the mid-19th century when it was cleared by the landowners. A few of the residents were relocated to purpose-built estate housing in Lamlash, while others sailed to begin new lives in Canada. A monument to the Arran Clearances stands on a green in front of estate cottages at Lamlash.

Follow the path across a concrete footbridge and climb to a path junction where a marker post indicates Meallach's Grave off to the right. Follow the clear albeit rougher path, climbing steeply for a short distance to reach this chambered cairn. Three tall stones are the visible remains of this ancient Clyde cairn, a type of chambered Neolithic tomb built to a pattern found across Argyll and southwest Scotland. Pottery sherds and glass beads recovered from the tomb during excavation in the 1960s are now in Glasgow's Hunterian Museum.

Retrace your steps from the cairn down to the waymarked path and continue along it to soon cross a footbridge over the Allt Lagriehesk. Turn left along the forestry road beyond, then left again after 400m onto a footpath once more. At a path junction, keep right, ignoring a path branching left across a footbridge, and descend alongside the Allt Lagriehesk to rejoin the outward route near the start.

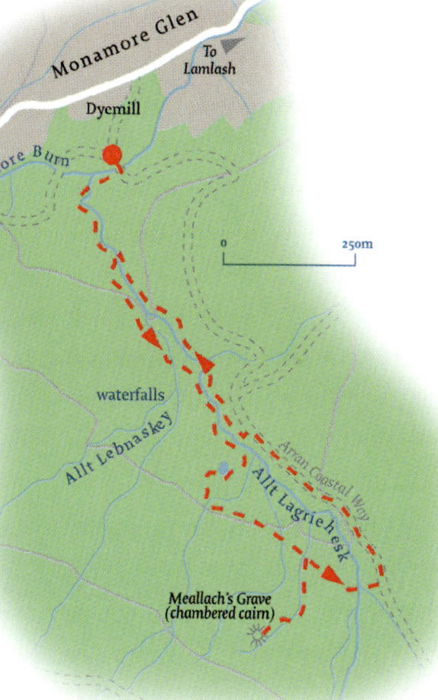


◂ Meallach's Grave

# Index